D1027113

PASS IT ON:
THE ENTREPRENEUR'S SUCCESSION PLAYBOOK

By

Harry M. McCabe

DISCLAIMER

This material was created to provide accurate and reliable information on the subjects covered. It is not intended to provide specific legal, tax, or other professional advice. The services of an appropriate professional should be sought regarding your individual situation.

These materials are not intended to be used to avoid tax penalties, and were prepared to support the promotion or marketing of the matter addressed in this document. The taxpayer should seek advice from an independent tax advisor.

Copyright © 2007 Harry M. McCabe
All Rights Reserved
Printed in the United States of America

McCabe, Harry M. 1952 -

ISBN: 978-0-9799123-0-6

This publication may not be reproduced, stored in a retrieval system or transmitted in whole or in part, in any form or by any means, electronic, mechanical, photocopying, recording, or otherwise, without the prior written consent of the Infinity Trust.

Infinity Trust
P. O. Box A 3039
Chicago, IL 60690

Publication date: October 1, 2007

This book is dedicated to

Christine, Jack, and **Mark,**

who remind me daily to love, nurture, and provide wisdom

in a fatherly way.

ACKNOWLEDGMENTS

This book was in my head, spread across my desk in countless files, and stored in bits and pieces on various computers for years. It would not have been completed without my writing coach, Frank W. Martin. He explained I had to start over and write from page one to the closing paragraph. He kept me on point through his knowledge and precision.

Special thanks go to my mentor, Uncle George, as well as my successor, youngest brother Mike. I'm truly blessed to modestly boast that Mike still handles some IRA rollover assets that our Dad planted as he set up pension plans in the 1960s. Succession, while at times turbulent, does work.

I also wish to acknowledge my past "A" clients, who taught me so much.

Finally, I extend sincere gratitude to my RADA and Partner/Protégé friends from across the country. We toiled and dreamt about the long-term. I'm grateful for you sharing your wisdom.

CONTENTS

PROLOGUE

I will never forget the evening of March 13, 1977. Then a twenty-four-year-old lieutenant in the United States Army, I studied for an exam as my wife wrote a letter to her parents about the day's activities in Landstuhl, Germany.

Suddenly, a loud knock on the front door of our apartment disturbed the peace and quiet of that Sunday night. I peered through the peephole of the door and saw an Army chaplain standing in the hallway. This startled me. Although I often received telephone calls and pages at different hours of the night as a duty officer, the presence of a chaplain indicated this was no ordinary problem.

I opened the door, and the chaplain firmly grasped my right hand. "I am so sorry," he said softly, "to tell you that your father passed away this morning."

Everything in my life changed at that moment. As the oldest son and his namesake, the news of my father's premature death shook and shocked me. So much of his life had been part of mine.

As a young boy, I watched him start his company and occasionally went to his office on weekends or in the evenings. I worked as an apprentice in the family business for nine months after graduating from St. Norbert College and prior to active service in the Army. During that wonderful nine-month period, I earned my first insurance licenses, and Dad formally brought me into Consolidated Pension Consultants (CPC).

He co-owned the business with his brother, George. I returned to live in the family home from May of 1974 until January of 1975, and Dad and I talked about the pension business from dawn to dusk.

By working under the direct supervision of Dad, I came to understand many aspects of the pension industry. We had similar personalities, but his management style and enthusiasm for life was—and still is—impossible to replicate. He complimented me often on my ability to understand complexities of business structures and the application of pension plan design and operation.

Yet he challenged me to be a sales expert rather than a technician. As in many small family businesses, our strong bond overcame obstacles in the business environment. We loved each other.

Dad often created training techniques on an impromptu basis. A comical example: As a young boy, I tried to complete my homework in a front office of Dad's general agent facility. He had gathered junior agents in the training room and wanted to impress upon them the need to bring enthusiasm to their work. But I kept hearing all kinds of racket from the training room.

So I stood in the hallway outside the room and watched a younger agent tapping the table with a Wiffleball™ bat. The training exercise was apparently designed to have the presenter emphasize his words by slamming the bat on the table. Then I observed another agent gently tapping the bat in his hand, which frustrated Dad.

He got up and demonstrated the enthusiasm he wanted by pounding the bat against the table. As he continued his presentation, his voice grew louder, and he hit the table harder with the bat. Then, at the conclusion, he hit the table so hard that the bat bent and went limp. The agents jumped to their feet and loudly applauded. Dad just smiled, knowing that he accomplished his goal.

Without question, Dad knew how to motivate people, but I think he took special pleasure in preparing me for the world and life in his company. However, since I had received a government-issued military draft lottery number of "6", I would spend a tour of duty in the United States Army and interrupt my training for a career at CPC.

To accelerate my training for the company, Dad decided to change my compensation from a small salary, which covered my rent payment to my parents for living in the family home, to a commission structure. Therefore, I needed to generate new business to meet my fixed obligations and better manage my cash flow. This development coincided with one of the most comical yet valuable training sessions I experienced under Dad's tutelage.

One hot August night he explained that I would need to be ready at 7:30 a.m. the next morning dressed in suit and tie. I didn't quite understand why he wanted me to do that since the temperature the next day was supposed to be in the upper nineties. The next morning instead of driving to the office in separate cars he also recommended that I join him in his vehicle. We headed in a direction opposite the office. When I asked him where we were going, he just said that I should relax.

After a short time, we arrived at an industrial park in a nearby suburb of Chicago. Dad handed me twenty-five brochures, explained that he would pick me up around three o'clock, and left me on the front curb of a small business. Then it occurred to me that this was a sales training day!

Unfortunately, I wore a dark blue suit. As the temperature rose and I walked from plant-to-plant asking for an appointment with the owner, I became quite a sight. I was unsure if the perspiration resulted from my nervousness or the hot temperature. But I learned how to identify each company's decision-makers and presented brochures to either human resource or accounting managers. Occasionally, the receptionist curtly explained that a sales call could be made "by appointment only."

As lunchtime approached, I invited a prospect out for a sandwich. Of course, he had to drive to the local restaurant, since I didn't have my car. I did, however, get a chance to explain the contents of the brochure and one annuity product. The prospect even asked me to provide a quote for the program.

When Dad returned to pick me up, I proudly presented the business cards that I had picked up at various businesses. I think Dad was glad to get the brochures out of the storeroom in the office and into circulation, but he knew I had learned a valuable lesson when I told him I would be able to pay the rent if I closed a deal with one of the companies I had pitched.

I later learned a great deal from Dad during a joint sales call at a skyscraper in Chicago's Loop. We arrived early, so we had time to check the building directory and verify the exact floor and suite number of the corporate offices. Then Dad motioned me to go back outside, and we proceeded to walk around the block. Since the meeting was scheduled to begin at eleven, we still had about fifteen minutes to kill before our appointment.

Dad wanted to give me a practical tip and explained that promptness was important. Since I'd grown up as his oldest son in the family, I knew that wasting time was one of Dad's pet peeves. During idle time, which included sitting in office reception rooms, Dad had a habit of his tapping the fingernails of his left hand in sequence from smallest to index finger.

The more his impatience grew, the more rapid the pace. He tapped the tabletop, the bicep on his right arm, or the top of the dashboard on the car. As a delay became longer, the rhythmic thumping of his fingers accelerated to the point where it almost sounded like a pack of racehorses pounding the track as they headed for the finish line. My mother often reminded him to slow down if the accelerated rhythmic tapping turned into loud thumping. If she was next to him,

Mom affectionately reached out and held his left hand and attempted to caress the fingers into silence. I witnessed some decent arm wrestling between them if Dad waited more than ten minutes!

For family outings, we all needed to be in the car promptly. My sister Cathy, the eldest of five children, helped the younger siblings be on time so we didn't receive the *look* from Dad. He just always wanted to be on time.

I, however, learned a secret about Dad as we walked around the block prior to our joint sales call in Chicago. He went on to explain that he didn't want to arrive early for a meeting because it might give the prospect the impression that he had nothing else scheduled before this meeting. Dad needed to convey that our time was as valuable as his.

Calling on prospects as well as clients in downtown Chicago excited me as a young salesman. Learning how to minimize the commute from the suburbs to the city, finding the right parking lots, and getting to meetings on time was a challenge. But one minor observation stuck with me: I was impressed when I found the name of the individual that I planned to see on the Executive Directory, often located in the lobby of a downtown office building. To me, this became a symbol of accomplishment and really meant that someone had climbed the corporate ladder.

The last time I saw Dad alive was September of 1976. He and Mom visited Germany to spend time with me and tour Europe. On the night before they were to return to the United States, Dad and I sat in the apartment after Mom and my wife retired for the evening. My tour would end in March of 1978, so we discussed my return to the family business as well as growth plans and expansion ideas.

Dad went out of his way to proudly explain that while visiting with my superior officers they had given rave reviews about my performance. Then, with a glass of Glenfiddich in his hand, he said I was better suited for a large organization and explained he would not be able to take me back as a consultant with the firm.

At the time, I was taking night classes to earn a masters degree in business administration. While holding one of my management textbooks, Dad explained that theories contained in the book would not work in his company. I was never certain why he did not think my training and personality would work in his company but privately reasoned that Dad was happy to have one son on his way to a career outside the business. That would leave a chance for his next son, my brother John, as well as four nephews to consider a career in the family business.

During my overseas assignment, I also became ambivalent about working for Dad. "I'm not so sure I want to work for your little company," I said during our final conversation. There were thousands of career opportunities, but I only had one Dad and didn't want any business-related matter to ever come between us. Little did I know I would never see him alive again.

I completed my tour of duty on March 9, 1978, and returned to Chicago for several job interviews. I had corresponded a few times with Uncle George, who seemed reluctant to make a permanent commitment about rejoining the family business. However, after I began my job search, I knew he wanted me to return because he began to match or exceed offers I received from other companies. It became apparent that having another McCabe at the company could be a win-win situation.

When I returned to CPC, I stepped right into Dad's shoes. I assumed responsibility for many of his clients, the majority of whom I had met for the first time three years earlier. They immediately accepted me as their representative to work on administration of their qualified retirement plans, and as my experience grew, I confidently gave them additional planning strategies and products to help them grow their companies. During this time, I also heard great stories about Dad from

6

clients and even got many laughs from them about the many similarities of working with father and son.

Equally important, Uncle George became my new mentor, and he pushed my continuing education and supported my studies at American College, where I earned the designation of Chartered Life Underwriter. George also provided leadership and guidance for the company, and our relationship was professional but interdependent.

He and CPC needed depth and a long-term commitment. Conversely, I desired a fast paced business environment coupled with growth opportunity. So I made joint appointments with George and learned his style, which provided another terrific training environment.

We even attended national training meetings together. The Pension Research Information Media of Exchange (PRIME), Retirement Administrators and Designers of America (RADA) and Provident Life and Accident Insurance Co. annual conventions also gave me access to many of the greatest minds in the pension and insurance industry. I was instantly accepted, and Dad's friends became my friends.

I also discovered **"the next generation"** of pension and insurance producers at these meetings. While the dads (in my case, Uncle George) attended the executive sessions, the sons held our own meetings. We shared stories about family business challenges and evolved into a support group that stretched across the country. Many from "the next generation" eventually became my closest friends.

Eventually, the sons made more presentations during the meetings, and we all saw a shift to "the next generation" was eminent. The open, cross sharing of ideas at these regularly scheduled events cultivated an atmosphere that aided my maturation in the industry.

Our family business changed again in 1980, when cousin Tim McCabe joined CPC after earning an undergraduate degree in accounting and becoming a CPA while working at a local savings-and-loan. He brought an analytical approach to our business and seemed perfect to build our investment management capabilities. Helped by a RADA member from Kansas City, Missouri, we launched an affiliation with a broker-dealer service with Tim as the lead.

Later that year, I learned that Uncle George and Tim had set up another company called McCabe and Associates. I wasn't brought into the discussion until they presented the new company logo, which included the Irish flag colors.

Uncle George then implemented a planning strategy known as retired lives reserve, a technique that allowed pre-funding of post-retirement term life insurance. This benefit plan highly rewarded older employees. When I became aware that one had been installed at CPC, I read the handwriting on the wall.

It was time for me to begin my own company. I approached George in April of 1982, explaining that I would like to depart and set up my own consulting/insurance/advisory firm within six months. After some thought, George agreed and assisted with the rollout.

I launched Retirement Programs Corporation (RPC) on October 1, 1982, at the age of twenty-nine and began a lifelong love affair with entrepreneurship.

A dear friend of mine once expressed entrepreneurship in a very profound way. We just completed high school, and the next chapters of our lives lay before us. I enrolled in college while Jack enlisted in the army. As I began my undergraduate studies in engineering, he went to Vietnam.

Jack spoke about the freedoms that life presented us in this way: "If we were born in the 1700s, we would surely have boarded a ship to leave the old country and explore the opportunities across the sea. If we were born in the mid 1800s, we naturally would have connected with a covered wagon and traveled west to see the continent. But we were born in the early 1950s. Man has been to the moon and explored the depths of the sea. So what is left for the young American male to explore?"

Jack believed it was entrepreneurship, the last unknown frontier left for the ambitious young American. Exploring unknown adventures in business allowed anyone an opportunity to take risks, create wealth, and provide for the common good.

As I began my American dream with the mission of helping private business owners accumulate wealth in qualified pension plans, I experienced firsthand the intricacies of owning and operating a private business.

Fortunately, I began RPC with a base of clients, many of whom had originally been Dad's. I learned from their experiences as they thought about retirement. Many companies had joint ownership with no family ties. Recognizing a company's legal structure was as important as knowing the real powerbrokers and who really did what in each company. This information became vital to my own business success.

In co-owned firms, senior partners needed to be bought out. We designed the timelines to help meet the needs of exiting shareholders as well as those who would continue to own the corporate structure.

The combination of these life experiences helped me understand the need for thorough exit planning. I also knew that a collaborative approach was necessary to deliver the strategies and products necessary to satisfy the current and future stakeholders. Legal and tax considerations also became important issues for me to address in retirement planning. Once again, I relied on the contemporaries of Dad and Uncle George, and they took extra time to explain how the real world of consulting worked in these sensitive areas. Having specialized knowledge and understanding of the legal and tax implications helped my business thrive. We staffed according and grew annual revenue.

Mike, my youngest brother, joined the firm in 1985. He had earned an undergraduate degree in accounting at the University of Illinois in 1983 and passed the CPA exam the same year. He didn't seem happy working as an internal auditor for a large national company, so I extended an invitation for him to join me in the practice and became his mentor. He understood his role as the internal support specialist as he learned the business. His responsibilities grew quickly, and we became a solid team working together.

We added lines of business, which included estate planning for business owners. I found great satisfaction in bringing solutions to my clients in an orderly fashion as they grew their businesses and accumulated wealth. Advising retired participants on how to take their pension or profit sharing distributions became an invaluable service that we provided.

Retirement is a critical time in one's life. The business owner, in particular, felt that the world was going too fast and that his services were no longer needed. The feeling of uselessness created great anxiety. Counseling individuals from the financial aspect was not enough, so I took a very personal approach with each retiree. They might be financially sound, but a feeling of hopelessness and emptiness often created anxiety and blurred their view of the future.

So a few years later, it became apparent that I needed to add more services for clients in the area of money management. I worked with Bob Westrick and his associate Chuck Neff and explored the idea of setting up a SEC-compliant registered investment advisor to help manage qualified plan assets as well as the personal funds of clients. In 1993, we formed WNA Investment Programs, Inc. (WNA).

Originally, I was to own one-half of the company, but late in the start-up stage I invited my brother Mike to participate as an owner. He contributed personal funds to help capitalize the new enterprise and in turn received one-fourth of the equity. I was proud to have him participate in the new company and see the change in his mindset from employee to owner. His management skills sharpened, and his role in the firm grew. I, indeed, groomed my successor.

In April of 1996, I woke up in a hospital bed after a serious illness and realized that in the best interest of my family, clients, employees, and yes, even myself, that I should step down from RPC and WNA. I planned to be out of the businesses in six months. I knew my partners would absorb the interest that I had in WNA, but the challenge was to prepare the larger company for transition.

So I conducted a private auction, and two outside firms signed confidentiality agreements and analyzed the client base and economics of RPC. At the same time, a third-party, Bob Murphy, expressed interest. He and my brother Mike had formed a partnership and submitted a bid on the business. So I had three offers to evaluate.

I decided on Mike and Bob after great deliberation. We utilized one attorney to structure the documents so that we could save legal fees and concluded the deal in December. We hosted a reception with more than one hundred clients, advisors, friends and family members to announce the change as I exited my business on a cold snowy night.

After a few months of recuperation, it was time for me to begin the next part of my career. I explored both industry-related and new opportunities and eventually took a position with The Partners Group in Austin, Texas, as vice president of member firm development. I traveled the country and helped Partners gain a larger market share of the members' insurance production. Using Chicago as a base of operations, I commiserated with my peers throughout the country and became their liaison to our independent producer network.

The Partners Group rapidly grew into an entity known as **Partners**Financial, and it along with fifty others became part of National Financial Partners Corp. (NFP). The official business plan for NFP called for an initial public offering. As a shareholder, I closely examined the process and participated in its development, which occurred in 2003. Then I left NFP to return to my roots helping private business owners develop their financial plans.

As part of my love and devotion to the American entrepreneurial spirit, I hope to encourage others to fulfill their dreams and plan for the future with their family members and successors. They need to face the challenge and think about the endgame. Business succession planning can be complicated, but my experience has taught me to be persistent. As my own story illustrates, succession planning works. You, too, can plan for a better future.

INTRODUCTION

Every American possesses boundless chances to create commercial transactions, and our democracy provides freedom for those who want to take a chance to put God-given talents into a system to create wealth.

But as we venture into the seventh year of the new millennium, the fascinating test of being the owner of a company will be your long-term survival.

Since most owners operate their businesses in the form of a corporation, the value of the enterprise can be transferred to a new owner through a retitling of stock transaction. In effect, the life of an incorporated business can be perpetual. The entity can be passed onto future owners who can lead the business in new directions.

Consider these statistics from a Arthur Anderson/Mass Mutual study presented by Joseph Astrachan, Ph. D., editor of *Family Business Review*, in 2003: More than thirty percent of all family owned businesses survive into the second generation; twelve percent will still be viable into the third generation, with three percent of all family businesses operating at fourth generation level and beyond.

Why such dismal results? My answer is simple: the lack of succession planning. The owners did not build on what they achieved. They worked hard, often making huge personal sacrifices. Not all of their ideas and inventions worked, but many did and could have been the springboard to lift them into retirement as they pass the company to successors who could take the business to the next level of success.

The planning process does not provide a "cure-all" for a privately owned business but rather provides a format to integrate and implement various solutions for succession. Let's be painfully blunt: the family structure, nature of the business, and goals and objectives will never be the same for any two family enterprises. I consider every privately owned business a family business. Everyone on the planet has a family history—some fractured, others solid, and still others with no heirs. But every owner has family.

No two families are identical, and every business is different. This distinctiveness makes providing universal answers impossible. Thus, we need a process that will be flexible enough to allow for the special situations of each privately owned business yet provide benchmarks to measure progress. Finally, it must have conclusion. A plan without a destination—an achievable goal—has no chance of success.

So let's explore the 7 Steps to Succession℠. This model takes the form of building an arch and begins with a willing business owner who is motivated to formulate a plan. Just as an arch is built from two sides, this process involves simultaneous construction from two sides. During construction, the structure must be supported until the final, uppermost part is properly secured.

This keystone symbolizes the focal point of working together to find the proper formula for the transfer of ownership from one owner to the next and will eventually provide the support for a freestanding structure. Upon completion, the arch will be unique since the components for every private business and family are so vastly different. At the same time, though, each building block of the arch has features that are similar to other arches because of the general nature of business and commerce.

I first used an arch model in 1998 when I worked at **Partners**Financial and was asked to design a program to help sustain a multi-generational member firm. We assembled a collaborative team comprised of our staff, contacts at core carrier vendors, and most importantly, interested member firms located throughout the country. We launched a Partner/Protégé program with the dual mission of fast-track training for sons and daughters of our member firms and developing a model for a succession plan. I began the initiative with an educational program and utilized the training facilities of New England Financial in Boston, Massachusetts.

A key element to our early success included a supportive environment where all participants were treated as peers. I also gave them my commitment to work as a liaison with **Partners**Financial. The young men and women were eager to advance their careers, and they formed a strong kinship based on the common denominator of working for their fathers. Many immediately recognized the need for a formal ownership transition plan but were naturally reluctant to approach their fathers.

The formation of the first father's meeting was somewhat of a challenge. For various reasons, owners hesitated to commit the time to properly address the topic. I consequently called on a few old and dear friends to mingle with other fathers who expressed interest in the meeting, and a total of nine volunteered to attend the first session.

Knowing I would need assistance with the facilitation, I also drew on the experience of yet another old friend. I first met Rhanda Salameh ten years earlier when I consulted on the potential implementation of an Employee Stock Ownership Plan (ESOP) at her grandfather's plant near Chicago. He became ill, and she arrived on the scene as the next-in-line family member. Her background was clinical social work, with very limited knowledge of the business world or details of her grandfather's personal estate plan.

Then I introduced Rhanda to a competent attorney in my network and her grandfather's CPA. Through a collaborative effort, we eliminated the ESOP plan and installed a qualified 401(k) profit sharing plan.

It had been a few years since I had seen Rhanda, who then operated a company called Dynamic Resolutions, but she liked the idea of co-facilitating the father's meeting to develop a model for succession planning. The first meeting took place in April of 1998 at the offices of American General Life Insurance Co. in Houston, Texas. As part of Rhanda's ice breaking technique, she tossed a wooden block model that needed to be assembled by the participants.

I observed the men working together to form an arch model, and then it occurred to me that we were at the early stage of something very special. During subsequent meetings with owners and their children, I established the 7 Steps to Succession[SM].

The example I will use for this arch model will be a family owned business with a founder/owner who wants to pass the enterprise to one of his children. As we explore the seven steps of this process in *Pass It On*, you will have to adjust to your own particular set of circumstances to the model.

You may find that several of building blocks will be easily adapted to your personal situation and others will be more difficult. The exercises that I will present should allow you to participate in your own planning process. My concept will pose tough questions, and only you can find the right answers to fit your needs

7 Steps to Succession℠ is a strategic thinking process that requires action at the board of directors' level. This concept can be used to design a retirement plan for any entrepreneur, but it also is a process that can be utilized by younger or middle-age owners who may wish to pass the baton to co-workers rather than family members. In reality, a succession plan should be an extension of your business plan. Famed investor Warren Buffett has said he never bought a business unless he knew how he was going to eventually sell it. You should view your situation the same way.

Some of what will be discussed in *Pass It On* can also be applied to family members in a larger business environment: a senior officer of a public company may have a child moving up the ladder within the organization, or large individual shareholders may want to use their influence to help family members obtain positions with opportunity for growth.

Simultaneously, sons and daughters of influential parents may have felt neglected in the family. Powerful executives and entrepreneurs, at times, do not find that time to tend to the needs of their children. Some leadership styles may carry over into family matters, and the dominant personality of the senior generation might cause communication lapses. Emotionally charged connections between the generations add complications in the day-to-day business environment.

But my seven-step plan will not solve tactical issues such as how to improve your business operational processes. You need to lift yourself out of the daily routine of your business for succession planning. I invite you to join me in a higher level of thinking to envision the future and answer the question of how you will pass the torch to your successor.

Let's begin the process. To build an arch, we must find solid (hopefully level) ground. Think of this as your core values, your personal family values, and the vision and mission of your business. As the successful founder, you created a profitable company that you are most proud of. It reflects your personality and culture. You are most confident of the goods and services provided to customers. You took risks to achieve the goals and have provided your employees work to support their families. The taxes you pay show your business is a good corporate citizen.

You're respected in the community and support many meaningful causes. Your successors hopefully understand the enormous commitment you have made to the business. If not, then you may not want to work with that particular person in building your succession plan. Passing the keys to the business often equates to the transfer of other values, too.

Especially in business, this meeting of the minds on core values is critically important. But sometimes we will discover underground tremors that are not readily noticeable when we begin the arch building process, and the weight of the structure can reveal soft spots that may need to be firmed up to keep the plan in place for the long-term. Family dynamics can ruin ownership succession. Proper family support, as you will see, increases the probability of success, and open lines of communication are critical to the process.

The arch model represents the Founder/Parent Generation (G-1) on the left side while the Successor Generation (G-2) represents the right side. The blocks will be assembled concurrently. We must place the cornerstones on solid ground and will complete your succession arch with the placement of last uppermost block — **the Keystone**.

Throughout the process we will continue to define key issues and address them. Various professional advisors will be used to support the structure as the assembly of the arch progresses. The building blocks of the model represent the most common components that need to be addressed. You may have several of the pieces of your plan already formulated; our task is to assemble them in a systematic process. Other parts will be created, crafted, and molded so the can be placed in the arch at the appropriate time.

The following chapters present a comprehensive description of the arch model, and my goal is to improve the chances that your company will survive to benefit future generations and successfully compete in the global economy.

CHAPTER ONE:

THE McCABE ARCH

The McCabe Arch, which features the 7 Steps to Succession[SM] process, evolved from my personal experience as an owner of several family businesses as well as my subsequent commitment to create a breakthrough for succession in those enterprises.

But working for **Partners**Financial as vice president of member firm development perfectly positioned me in the late 1990s to interact with many multi-generational firms and was a natural place for me to develop a succession plan theory by creating an environment for learning from two—and sometimes three—generations of business owners who shared their successes, failures, dreams, and concepts of retirement.

In April of 1998, I gathered nine fathers who owned and operated financial consulting and insurance distribution firms to form a study group dedicated to the sole issue of "passing the torch" to a successor. The group became known as "The Houston Nine" because this groundbreaking meeting took place at the American General Life Insurance Co. in Houston, Texas.

Rhanda Salameh of Dynamic Resolutions served as my co-facilitator for this eighteen-month program. Later, she decided to use a questionnaire to evaluate relationships, and I arranged to use the New England Financial agent-training program to identify the major concerns of business owners in choosing the proper successor and leaving the business.

We refined the father's training program in 2001 when we conducted a second study group, dubbed "The Atlanta Eleven" because we met in the capital of Georgia. In addition to the training tools used in the first study group, we included a book entitled *How to Run Your*

Business So You Can Leave It in Style by John Brown, which added different checklists and materials for our discussions.

Through humorous but firm cajoling, Rhanda and I fine-tuned our conversations with the groups and identified the issues most important to these fathers: family, management and ownership of the business, and concern about certain daily operations in the enterprises.

For example, the fathers wanted to know if their spouses or family members not involved in the business should be involved in our meetings about succession, the dynamics of leadership with multiple second generation protégés, and health issues—either the health of the founding generation or the second generation.

Succession Plan Time Table

STEP	DESCRIPTION	MONTH
1	Recognize need – Pre group formation and screening	1-3
2	First Meeting of G1; Gather group consensus – introduce model 21 Factor questionnaire	4
3	Conference call – report to members on goals and actions G2 members will attend separate Educational retreat Through a facilitated use of distance learning member firms identify issues and solve with open communication	6
4	Second meeting for G1- introduce tools for conflict resolution- draft written plan for crisis – shared Knowledge & Practical implications	9
5	Conference call – with both G1 & G2 – Goals and Key issues – Collective Wisdom	12
6	Group meeting with G1 and G2 – team building and cross-mentoring opportunities.	14
7	Web Conference call for all – testimonials - link to continuing implementation of Plans	18
	Maintain focus and progress reporting through Keystone event	

Management and ownership issues included establishing a target date when the founder would retire, how to deal with co-owners holding a minority interest, the role of non-family managers, and understanding the provisions of life insurance agency contracts and vested renewal compensation.

Finally, the fathers considered daily operations of the company that effected present and future profitability, including product line focus, client service, internal technology development, employee training, and revenue sharing.

We constantly looked for additional key issues that needed to be addressed. For instance, we tried to role play what it would be like to pass ownership to a son and son-in-law of the founder and imagine what the conversation around the Thanksgiving table might be when problems in the business surfaced.

To complicate matters, the founders often commented that they really never would fully retire from the business. This, of course, brought muffled groans from the protégés and highlighted how difficult passing the torch really can be if an ironclad agreement for succession isn't worked out.

Later, during a meeting devoted to the topic of crisis management, we began with the fathers in one room and the protégés in a separate location. Then we combined the two groups in one room, and I wrote "Dad died yesterday" on a flip chart. That immediately got everybody's attention. Then I asked the protégés, "What would you do first?"

From an emotional point of view, watching parents intently listen to their offspring added great depth as well as a sense of mortality and seriousness to the session. Suddenly, everyone understood nothing lasts forever, and thinking and planning for the unthinkable was a prudent but highly challenging task—one that was much more difficult than just discussing the ramifications of life insurance policy design.

Key issues varied from participant to participant in our various meetings, but the most important seemed to be how each person finally addressed their own special issues. Over the eighteen months of the program, each owner resolved his key issues through open dialogue with the protégé and support of the group.

Time became an important factor in the process. In one situation, for instance, the father was not ready to address a succession plan since a younger son still attended college. He felt strongly that the personality of this younger son would fit well into the business. Consequently, he decided to put the succession decision on hold for a few years while he actively continued to support his older son, who was already working at the company and developing his technical and managerial skills.

In another case, the protégé was a woman. While she continued to take on more responsibility at the firm and had a strong desire to someday be the owner, she took time off to raise her own children. Her father, who was delighted to be a grandfather, supported her decision and put the company's succession plan on hold until his daughter rejoined the firm on a full-time basis.

These—and many other situations—allowed me to understand that each step in the succession process must be flexible enough to permit customization for individual companies. This realization became critical to my approach. Each firm had different issues, and, of course, each family had its own dynamics. I outlined a seven-step process with descriptions of activities in each step. Initially, I began at the top of the page and worked in a tabular format from top to bottom. This seemed natural and helped everyone understand the original model.

Cornerstone Parent /Founder	Blocks	Cornerstone Next generation successor
Business is a going concern	1	Identified family member who is committed to business – outside experience successes - basic sales and licensing
Economic review: determination if retirement plan sufficient to support lifestyle	2	Formal Education complete: BBA or MBA– Industry training – Credentials, Competence specialization
Business plan: orderly transfer of clients	3	Build client base: specialization & core competencies emerge
Crisis Plan: written plan for Death and Disability of senior owner with commitment to second generation repurchases.	4	Crisis Plan: commitment to honor terms of agreement – provide reciprocal provisions.
Reengagement plan: Will activities and hobbies really make the retirement fulfilling?	5	Shouldering the weight of leadership: Successor responsibilities grow and industry contacts development
Estate Plan: Make decisions on equalization for non-business family members, special grants and Philanthropic goals.	6	Marketing Plan: Sales and Production to demonstrate responsibilities that include cash flow and profitability.
Letting go: Issues openly reviewed with final	7	Final Documentation: Legal and operational authority transferred

Without question, we needed to introduce the succession planning process as a simple concept with obtainable and measurable results. It was imperative for the stakeholders to immerse themselves in the process for it to work effectively. Given the need for flexibility and creativity, we also interjected activities that led to working with multi-generational issues in a relaxed environment and experimented with a few techniques to open lines of communication as we built the model. This included sessions exclusively for the fathers, others exclusively for the successors, and still more as joint meetings.

One of the more lively exchanges occurred during a retreat late in the seven-step process of "The Houston Nine." Both generations attended segregated sessions during the day, and then we arranged for a twenty-five person private bus to transport us to dinner. As we loaded the bus, I determined seat assignments. Each father sat with a next-generation protégé other than his own.

Then I assigned a topic for discussion: How do you pass a client relationship from the father to the protégé? After all, the orderly transfer of business relationships in the service industry is a key issue for everyone. When allowed to openly discuss the question with the nine parents, the comments from the protégés ranged from "just get dad out of the way" to "I cannot make any money on the prospects you give me."

The forty-five minute ride turned out to be one of the loudest, upbeat sessions of the day. It was utterly fascinating to watch the role reversal as the senior generation listened intently to the comments of the protégé.

At other group meetings and educational retreats, I employed a game that I personally experienced as a member of PRIME and RADA study groups. To diffuse tension with founders and protégés, I invited them play an easy, low-stakes card game entitled "99" with a winner-take-all format.

The participants built camaraderie and learned important lessons about the competitive nature of everyone at the table. During these games, people also said things that got to the heart of the succession problem in a comical way. Consequently, it became easier for me to help clear the roadblocks and keep the founders and protégés on an upbeat path to a succession plan.

In a different setting, we discussed joint sales calls by the parent and protégé, which provided humorous examples about how clients viewed the sales process. For instance, one father asked his protégé to develop a presentation for a new product line to supplement existing insurance coverage for a long-time client. Then they booked a meeting to explain the new product at the client's office. After the initial introductions, the protégé began the presentation in a professional and detailed manner. The client smiled, looked at his watch, made eye contact with the father, interrupted the presentation by telling the protégé that he would buy the product, and then asked for the application so he could sign and close the deal.

The father didn't give the protégé a chance to respond and asked everyone out for lunch. Back in the office later that afternoon, the protégé discussed the sales call with his father, and both generations learned tough lessons about trust and passing the torch.

At one point in the discussion on joint sales calls, I also shared my own experiences working with Uncle George in the family pension consulting business. I had been so eager to please clients that I over-prepared, and the computer-generated illustrations I presented just overwhelmed everyone. George recognized the need for me to simplify my presentation and reigned me in, more or less telling me to streamline my materials. On other occasions, I knew that we closed business based on long-standing and trusted relations with clients who were owners of private companies. I simply had to acknowledge the fact and move on without feeling insecure. Each of us had a strong personality and desire to provide the best long-term solutions for the client. We had to accept each other's style, strengths, and weaknesses.

Throughout the eighteen-month "Houston Nine" program, my mind constantly flashed back to the wooden block model that Rhanda had earlier used for an icebreaker exercise at the initial meeting. Later, I purchased a model to illustrate the step-by-step process for a building a succession plan and began to rethink how this seven-step process could be translated into a one-on-one process. The concept of a visual arch model intrigued me, and I committed extra time to developing a plan for succession using an arch model that worked.

You can think about models from many different viewpoints. We all probably remember constructing a model as a child. In my case, I built model airplanes. The steps needed to assemble a model led me think I could also build a process for something as emotional and intangible as succession.

In the building construction world, builders start at the bottom and work upward. When the arch model began to crystallize in my mind, this process seemed to be a more natural visual concept for many reasons. When you build an airplane, for example, you often construct many of the components before final assembly. The same is true with the different components of an arch.

However, the unique aspect of an arch was that we continually build it from two sides. For a succession planning model to work, we needed commitment from the owner and the protégé. It was imperative that both sides complete their assignments with the ultimate goal of the finding—and resolving—the key issues that were represented by the various blocks.

The most important issue would be closure and is represented by the Keystone, which was the uppermost block placed in the model and holds it together. The scaffolding could only be removed when the Keystone was permanently secured.

The McCabe Arch & 7 Steps to Succession[SM]

PARENT /FOUNDER (G-1)	STEP	SUCCESSOR GENERATION (G-2)
Letting go: Issues openly completed with final action.	7	**Final Documentation:** Legal and operational authority transferred.
Estate Plan: Make decisions on equalization for non-business family members, special grants and Philanthropic goals.	6	**Business Plan:** Sales and Production to demonstrate responsibilities that include cash flow and profitability.
Reengagement plan: Will activities and hobbies really make the retirement fulfilling?	5	**Shouldering the weight:** Successor leadership responsibilities grow and industry contacts development
Crisis Plan: Written plan for Death and Disability of senior owner with commitment to next generation ownership purchase	4	**Crisis Plan:** Commitment to honor terms of Buy/Sell agreement – funded to provide reciprocal provisions.
Marketing Plan: Orderly transfer of clients	3	**Build client base:** Specialization & core competencies emerge
Economic review: Determination if projected assets are sufficient to support lifestyle	2	**Formal Education:** BBA and Industry training – Credentials to demonstrate competence & specialization
Business: A profitable going concern	1	Identified **Family Member(s)** who are committed to business
Cornerstone	↑	**Cornerstone**

When I converted the seven step-by-step succession planning process from a top down style to a bottom-up table and named the blocks for each side, The McCabe Arch with the 7 Steps to Succession[SM] became a working model that could be custom-built to accommodate the needs of any private business.

As I refined the bottom-up table, I transferred my thoughts and notes into a presentation, allowing me to assemble the wooden blocks and providing descriptions for each step. I immediately cultivated the interest of my audience whether it was a small group or one-on-one setting, and I saw that I had struck a nerve.

But some business owners still resisted the process when I put all fifteen blocks on the table. An owner once rolled eyes, smiled, and said, "This is complicated, and I've got most of this done."

I responded, "Have you ever seen it completely assembled?

He gestured that I should proceed, and my presentation provided the catalyst for him to eventually use my succession planning process, and we have made great progress toward plan completion.

In other one-on-one presentations, I get interrupted often when I insert a particular block into the model. For example, I'm stopped at Step Four when an owner wanted to tell his story about buying out the heirs of a deceased partner. In another case, I observed a client shake his head negatively in the early steps as I placed the blocks for the successor generation. Since I always make a mental note of these reactions during the presentation, I asked questions pertaining to the development of the successor.

Another time, I placed the founder block in Step Five with the successor present. I noticed an inquisitive expression on the face of the founder and noted the comments and reactions as I placed this vital component. I stopped the presentation to referee the heated discussion between the generations.

I also drew on my experience as a pension consultant to closely held business owners to help answer question like "How do I get Dad to retire?" I suggested that the company throw a retirement party. It then became public knowledge to suppliers, bankers, employees, and most importantly, the clients. All the details for the official stock transfer may not have taken place, but it put a timed benchmark on the calendar.

A few years ago, I visited the St. Louis arch and studied the exhibits leading up to the entrance, finding the descriptions of the landmark helpful to my own arch and the work I did on behalf of private business owners. One exhibit was remarkable in its simplicity, and I recommend that you do the following exercise before embarking on the succession journey:

Take a piece of small chain about three feet long, and hold it in front of your body. Slowly move your hands together and see how the arch is formed upside down. Every arch has its own slope and forms a distinct shape depending on the size and structure of the links.

This principle is true in succession planning. Each situation is different. As your succession blocks are assembled, they begin to lean towards each other. But the process fails without proper support and commitment. One of the most crucial elements of succession planning is determination. As my Uncle George often said, "The best thing that Christopher Columbus ever did was start."

Planning for your departure as a founder must contain a strong commitment to build a better future for yourself and your company.

That can happen if you use 7 Steps to Succession℠ in The McCabe Arch as a process to coordinate the personal, legal, and financial issues that need to be addressed before you pass on your legacy to the next generation.

CHAPTER TWO:

FOUNDATION

I served on the steering committee for the Family Firm Institute (FFI) International Convention that was held on October 19-22, 2005, in Chicago, with an official theme of Varied Architectures: The Art and Science of Designing Family Enterprises. For a better perspective of Chicago's rich history and architectural heritage, FFI suggested that attendees read *The Devil and the White City*, a national bestseller by Erik Larson. After reading the book, I fixated on a striking passage describing the foundation needed to support the Montauk Building, an early Chicago skyscraper:

"The trickiest part of the Montauk was its foundation. Initially, Mr. Root (the architect) planned to employ a technique that Chicago architects had used since 1873, to support buildings of ordinary stature. Workers would erect pyramids of stone on the basement slab. The broad bottom of each pyramid spread the load and reduced settlement; the narrow top supported load bearing columns. To hold up ten stories of stone and brick, however, the pyramids would have to be immense, the basement transformed into a Ginza of stone. (The developer) Mr. Brooks objected....

"... The solution, when Mr. Root first struck it, must have seemed too simple to be real. He envisioned digging down to the first reasonably firm layer of clay, known as hard-pan, and there spreading a pad of concrete nearly 2 feet thick. On top of this workers would set down a layer of steel rails, stretching from one end of the pad to the other and over this a second layer, at right angels. Succeeding layers would be arranged the same way. Once complete, this *grillage* of steel would be filled and covered with cement to produce a broad, rigid raft that he called a floating foundation. What he was proposing, in a fact, was a stratum of artificial bedrock that would also serve as the floor of the basement. Mr. Brooks liked it."

I, too, like the concept for succession planning. For many years, I have discussed the foundation on which to build The McCabe Arch with its 7 Steps to Succession℠. My definition included core personal values of the business owner, the family values that he or she had hoped to pass on to future generations of family members, and then intertwined all these values with the business mission, vision, and purpose. I referred to this as the "fiber of the culture" in which the true beliefs of the business owner must be initially identified, developed, and communicated to form the solid foundation on which we begin the succession planning process.

But to begin my process, you must dig below the surface to find the true values from different directions. Financial, spiritual, and emotional values as well as business philosophy, profit motive, and management style will be the components of the foundation. It needs to be strong enough to support change, accept pressure, and stand the test of time.

I often flesh out these values by asking private business owners the following two questions: How important is it for you to leave a legacy? If it is important, what is the legacy?

A few owners often shrug and coldly say, "Why do I care, I'll be dead."

Others will nod with a smile and say, "I've been doing a lot of thinking about this and have some ideas."

Still others simply produce a buy-sell agreement or a Last Will and Testament documenting what they feel is their succession plan.

Entrepreneurs are truly unique individuals, and that's why I enjoy my work so much. Each company's succession circumstance is different, resulting in diverse and challenging consulting assignments for me.

Bill Bachrach, CSP, is a highly regarded author for the financial services industry and a big proponent of value-based thinking. He encourages financial advisors, insurance sales agents, and investment representatives to begin their process with a dialogue about what is really important for the prospect or client.

One of the first questions he says they should ask: "What is important about money to you?" The key word is "important." When the question is asked properly, the respondent is encouraged to think below the surface and search for the more valuable emotional underpinnings of the question. Based on the answer, Bachrach assists advisors and agents on how to proceed to the next step in the selling process.

Likewise, the succession consultant can begin to search for below-the-surface elements of relationships, expected behavior, leadership, and attitudes toward wealth. This becomes a very personal process because the consultant must often ask questions like, How does one balance the love and work equation? and Does the family's faith conflict with the ethics practiced in the business?

Author Ellen Frankenberg, Ph.D., states in her book *Your Family Inc.* that each generation has to redefine the family mission. "As the family firm matures and become successful, the mission of the family shifts from surviving to sustaining and, eventually to transmitting great wealth. The role of children also shifts from being low-cost helpers to becoming the recipients of great wealth..."

Determining the attitude of various family members toward wealth, ownership, and control will be developed during the arch building process. These values are based on family traditions, and I encourage my clients to tell stories about family vacations and trips with the kids away from the office. The stories can vividly express many core values.

For example, I recall a family camping trip with my mother and father and four siblings. Our station wagon pulled a pop-up camper through the mountains of Colorado. One drive, in particular, began to put a strain on our capacity to sit still. My father searched for a campground that we had picked out of a camping guide. Dusk hit as we continued to make hairpin turns along the narrow road, and we took a wrong turn.

At that point, the headlights failed to work, and suddenly it was pitch black. My father's first directive to me was to sit on the hood and shine a flashlight on the road so we could maneuver. I was probably twelve years old and never before sat on the front of a moving vehicle with a flashlight overlooking a steep cliff. The improvisation worked, and we safely arrived at the campsite.

As the children set up the pop-up tent, I noticed my father and mother debating the prudence of my prior activity. Then we established the campsite and started a campfire, and Dad leaned over to me and apologized for putting me in jeopardy. I thought that sitting on the hood was just part of the adventure, and then I realized how frightened I really was. This story, however, illustrates that both Dad and I took risks when the situation warranted such action.

Private business owners can easily identify their core motivational values courtesy of an exercise provided by www.2164.net, which is a division of the Andrea and Charles Bronfman Philanthropies. Prioritize the following values to help you determine your foundation:

- Freedom-embracing liberty: exercising choice and free will;

- Spiritual Growth-seeking to connect to a higher purpose;

- Competence –being effective at what you do;

- Leadership-guiding people and projects: setting the pace;

- Helping-taking care of others and meeting their needs;
- Responsibility-voluntarily doing the what is expected of you;
- Courage-standing up for your beliefs;
- Justice-pursuing what is fair and morally right;
- Community-feeling a meaningful connection to a group of people;
- Pleasure-seeking personal enjoyment and fun;
- Personal Growth-pursuing new skills and self awareness;
- Tradition-respecting an established way of how things have been done;
- Power-having the ability to influence others;
- Friendship-experiencing close, ongoing relationships;
- Equality-respecting everyone's right to parity;
- Tolerance-being open to different ideas;
- Obligation-committing to fulfill a duty or promise;
- Belonging-feeling connected to and liked by others;
- Family-taking care of and spending time with love ones;
- Integrity-adhering to own moral or ethical code;
- Innovation-finding new and creative ways of doing things;
- Compassion-feeling sympathy, care, or concern for others;
- Opportunity-having the chance to experience progress and advancement;
- Recognition-getting noticed for your efforts;
- Risk-exploring the unknown and testing limits.

In comparison to Root's broad but artificial bedrock foundation for the Montauk Building, the foundation for a family business is **real**, not artificial. People, however, experience the same activity from a different perspective. A child's view of an event will be totally different than the parents. During multi-generational dialogue, we identify these different perspectives. In succession planning, neither will be incorrect, but it's important to recognize these variables to allow flexibility in future discussions.

When a professional consultant attempts to understand the true values of clients, different questioning techniques can be used. For example, statements requiring a true and false response might be helpful. Another style may be to rank a written list of attributes from high to low. Recalling a life event or storytelling may also be useful.

I, however, recommend that clients write their responses. This forces them to use a different part of the brain. In addition to formulation of the answer, this method triggers the use of hand muscles to move the writing instrument. I've been told this helps to demonstrate more commitment to the response. By using workbooks that contain a variety of questionnaires, I also try to use multiple styles, and, at times, clients complain that I'm being redundant.

At other times, I ask a provocative question to get what I need about core values. "Have you ever had surgery?" I say with a smile and then explain the following series of events:

I had torn a rotator cuff and needed outpatient arthroscopic surgery in my shoulder. General anesthesia would be used to knock me out for a short period of time. A few days before the procedure, I went to the outpatient registration desk to complete the paperwork and necessary insurance pre-certification. As I left the office, I was given a list of instructions and counseled by one of the volunteers. I was told not to eat anything after midnight prior to the 4:00 p.m. scheduled operation.

The day of the procedure, I went to work for a few hours in the morning. It was a warm summer day, so I decided to enjoy the weather and took a walk in the forest preserves of suburban Chicago. But I still had time to kill before leaving for the hospital, and I went home, started the lawnmower, and cut the grass. Then I cleaned up and prepared myself for the late afternoon event.

Upon arriving at a hospital, the receptionist pulled my file and asked me a laundry list of questions to make sure that I was the right patient for the right procedure. She also asked about prescription medications, home phone number, and what I ate that day. The next stop was a nurse's station, where they asked additional questions about my height, weight, and allergies to medicine.

Again, they asked me what I ate or drank. They escorted me to a waiting area and gave me a surgical gown. After changing in a small locker room, I climbed aboard a surgical gurney, where nurses gave me an injection and shaved my shoulder. The technician again asked me again about the medications I took, allergies, etc. They also wanted phone numbers of family members that would be available to drive me home if I needed assistance. This all seemed reasonable since I had been through other outpatient medical procedures.

The doctor stopped by, and we chatted. He asked me again if I was ready, how I felt, and when was the last time I had any food or drink. I said that I had a glass of water about two o'clock in the afternoon. At that point, he looked at the head nurse with great frustration and told me that we had to reschedule the procedure. The reason was, of course, that I had consumed fluids and the anesthesiologist would not be able to appropriately administer the medication with water in my system.

I, too, became agitated that I was allowed to get this far in the process. But, on reflection, I noted the way different individuals phrased their questions, their tone of voice, and their delivery method. I just didn't hear the "drink" part of most questions, but the doctor asked me in a manner that brought out the correct answer.

Questioning at different times by different people is similar to the steel bars placed in the floating foundation of a building. People ask questions different ways from different directions and from diverse points of view. Dissimilar questioning techniques may be utilized in the succession planning process by trusted advisors as they attempt to help the client to determine their core values and the issues that need to be resolved.

Additionally, the values of owners are an accumulation of outside influences beginning with whom they played with as a child. Think, for a moment, about how a community constantly influences values. As a parade comes down Main Street, do the onlookers salute the American flag as the color guard passes by? Does the Sunday church community start service on time? Or does one even belong to a church community? Questions about attending a condominium homeowners meeting voluntarily and abiding by the rules might also demonstrate core values. The ethics of a community and its leaders influence the development of children, and the behavior of adults, too.

However, other key players must also involve themselves in a collaborative manner to produce a workable succession plan. Close advisors—typically a CPA, attorney, and tax consultant—must assist the business owner in setting an agenda so the relevant topics are timely and properly addressed. For example, the initial succession meeting usually includes the owner, CPA, designated successor, and me in an informal gathering where the primary objective is to confirm the commitment of time and resources from all parties to the succession planning process.

Business literature and academics continually stress the importance of vision and mission for any enterprise. Quite simply, successful private companies clearly express their purpose. When conducting research on a company, I often look at its Web site for the terms "client" versus "customer" to determine the type of relationship the company encourages. I also look for a mission statement to determine what the written direction of the enterprise might be. Marketing slogans and tag lines also give an indication of the corporate culture, and this information can be overlaid and made part of the foundation.

∞ ∞ ∞ ∞

The challenges of creating a succession plan are greater when family members are not interested in continuing the business, and the owner may need to dig deeper to create a guaranteed "market" for his business interest. It is also imperative to allow those who are interested in continuing the business to do so without interference from the heirs of a deceased owner.

Moreover, the succession plan should establish the market value of the business and provide liquidity for the estate of the deceased owner while the mission of the business must be preserved to ensure the desired legacy and continued opportunity for financial success of the new owner.

The foundation of a non-family succession plan will help protect the financial interests of the business and all those connected to it. If something were to happen to a key employee or owner, the plan must provide the business with funds to help everyone through rough financial patches or allow time to search for the replacement of a key employee. I'm not suggesting that a vault needs to be installed to horde cash, but contingency reserves should be set aside for emergencies.

Other questions to be considered in non-family succession planning:

> Is the company strong enough to remain competitive or does it require a major overhaul of its products and services?

> Will the financial requirements of owner's family prevent the company from taking advantage of new market opportunities?

> Will the new owner obtain the amenities that he or she feels entitled to but hasn't yet earned?

> Is co-leadership acceptable to all candidates?

> Is the company's mission statement, clear enough to keep key employees on the job with a shared vision for the future?

There are many other indicators that can define core values. I ran into one of the most unique when I was on a business trip a few years ago and stayed at a Signature Inn. I'm a seasoned road warrior and consider a room more for its location than its amenities. After checking in at the front desk and receiving the room key, I settled into the modest accommodations and immediately found small a card that read:

> "To Our Guests,
>
> "In ancient times, there was a prayer for 'The Stranger within our gates.' Because this motel is a human institution to serve people, and not solely a moneymaking organization, we hope that God will grant you peace and rest while you are under our roof.
>
> "May this room and motel be your 'second' home. May those you love be near you in thoughts and dreams. Even though we may not get to know you, we hope that you will be as comfortable and happy as if you were in your own house.
>
> "May the business that brought you our way prosper. May every call you make, and every message you receive add to your joy. When you leave, may your journey be safe.
>
> "We are all travelers. From birth 'till death, we travel between the eternities. May these days be pleasant for you, profitable for society, helpful for those you meet, and a joy to those who know and love you best.
>
> Bill Haling, General Manager."

Talk about a mission statement! The general manager expressed his moral fiber in a highly unusual way. I felt comforted in his establishment that night. The next morning, I left an over-generous tip for the maid, kept the card, and still use it today as a bookmark.

CHAPTER THREE:

CORNERSTONES

With a foundation solidly embedded in the core values of a company, placing the cornerstones of The McCabe Arch is the first phase of the 7 Steps to Succession℠ process.

The cornerstone for the founder, which I refer to as the Generation One (G-1), symbolizes a profitable business entity that can grow over time, and further represents the founder's commitment to actively pursue a plan that results in the transfer of management and control of the company.

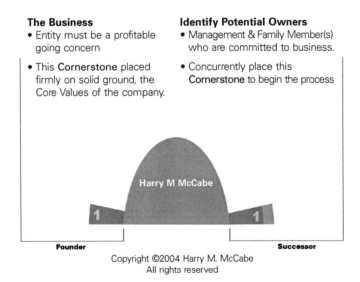

The Business
- Entity must be a profitable going concern
- This **Cornerstone** placed firmly on solid ground, the Core Values of the company.

Identify Potential Owners
- Management & Family Member(s) who are committed to business.
- Concurrently place this **Cornerstone** to begin the process

Harry M McCabe

Founder   Successor

Copyright ©2004 Harry M. McCabe
All rights reserved

The cornerstone for the successor generation, which I call the Successor Generation (G-2), represents the potential owners for this model. This block can contain one or multiple individuals from the family or the key employee group. For simplicity, we will define this cornerstone with one individual who is strongly committed to the company and has a vested interest in the completion of a succession plan.

When I speak of a profitable ongoing concern, I look for positive cash flow and a solid balance sheet coupled with a business plan that offers *real* attainable goals. These elements must be contained in the G-1 Cornerstone. Many private business owners choose to operate as a corporation with shares of stock that can be transferred and have chosen the subchapter "S" tax election. In other cases, owners structure their business as a partnership or sole proprietorship that might need to be restructured so it can be passed on.

The shape of the cornerstones must also be fully considered at this juncture of the planning process, especially the Successor Generation's commitment to the business and understanding of its economics. Five critical questions must be asked:

1) Do they understand the future growth potential and market position to remain competitive?
2) Will the company require an upgrade of its product line?
3) Do the successors understand the importance of the business to other family members as well as the community?
4) Can they really make a contribution to the ongoing success of the business?
5) If, by chance, there are co-successors, can they peacefully co-exist and establish a unified leadership and management team?

Likewise, the size of cornerstones will vary greatly depending on the value of the company. Determining the value of a business is a fascinating science and can be the most difficult and time-consuming aspect of succession planning. When I decided to sell Retirement Programs Corporation in 1996, I visualized the process as an intricate puzzle that I had to assemble based on:

Size in terms of employees;

Expense associated with overhead;

Breath of the customer base;

Physical location of company and customers;

Access to capital markets;

Key executive dependency;

Service and product lines;

Litigation/regulatory risk;

Volatility of the industry.

Then I put the pieces of my puzzle together and forecasted the recurring revenue stream to determine a reasonable value of my consulting practice. In the sale of my own company, this procedure worked well for uninterrupted service to my loyal clients, my successor, and my future endeavors.

When designing a succession plan for family members or key employees, we often shrink the value of the business. This minimum defensible value can then be used for gift tax purposes in the event that inter-generational gifts will be part of the solution. Equally important, the successor may not have sufficient ready cash to do a large transaction, so the terms of the sale will need to be adjusted to meet those needs.

Once we identify the component parts of the cornerstones, where should we place them? Each company arch will have its own slope and individual design, so you must think about the existing relationship between the current owner and the successor. When a close working or loving relationship exists between owner and successor, the cornerstones may be placed closer together to create informal and formal lines of communication to satisfy the desires of each party.

The participants may be able to support themselves (imagine a tall but narrow archway) during the process. They may have little need for their trusted outside advisors, who simply surround the arch and provide assistance on technical matters.

Unfortunately, there could be pre-conceived notions of the outcome of any succession plan, especially if the founder has repeatedly said "someday this all will be yours" to a family member or key employee. This unofficial perception of ownership may cause operational problems for the company during the owner's control of the company as well as during succession plan implementation if the expectations are unfulfilled.

There may also be unforeseen problems on the founder's side of the equation, ranging from a dominating personality where self-esteem is gained from running the business to just plain greed. They often resist opening up the "box" to reveal the total compensation and benefit package. Each side must work together to define the issues that need to be solved as the cornerstones are properly constructed. If the owner and successor are far apart on their expectations, we may need to place the cornerstones further apart.

Both sides will be asked to stretch and identify their ultimate goals in order to reach a consensus. Trusted advisors, who have stood on the sidelines, may now be used to help create a consensus between the owner and the successor or may even point to exactly where the cornerstones are placed.

But who, really, should be included as a trusted advisor on the owner's succession planning team?

Strategic policy decisions normally are made at the board level in larger companies yet many private business owners and entrepreneurs do not have a formal board of directors or even an informal advisory board. The challenge, therefore, is to assemble the right team of specialists because proper professional counsel is paramount to the succession planning process.

Each profession has its own credentialing procedures and code of ethics and most professions require continuing education and training. An owner may have used one or all of the following advisors independently in conducting daily business operations and now may have to rely on their judgment in making critical decisions about the transfer of ownership:

- **Certified Public Accountant (CPA).** Normally, the CPA is the most trusted financial advisor for small business owners. Studies consistently verify this fact. My explanation: The CPA provides financial benchmarks on a routine basis, and usually completes the owner's annual individual and business tax returns. Sitting with the CPA often is the only time the business owner reviews organized financial reports that can be compared to past years. CPAs are typically an accountant who documents what has happened in the business. They look backwards and compile financial results that are required by various taxing bodies. Consistency of the relationship is deepened by the interpretations of the tax code as it applies to the client situation. By nature, the entrepreneur tends to be more aggressive in positioning financial accounts to minimize the tax impact, but the CPA keeps the owner within current guidelines and requirements. This annual ritual deepens their bond and generally makes the relationship the strongest among professional advisors.

- **Banker.** This resource may be one of the most misunderstood relationships in the business community. A bank provides loans, for various reasons, that are essential to a growing business. For the mature, successful business an established line of credit keeps cash flow moving efficiently during natural business cycles. Long-term expansion projects financed with corresponding long-term debt helps the entrepreneur leverage business efficiencies. On the other hand, banks need to evaluate their loan risks and monitor the profitability of their clients. The use of personal guarantees to secure appropriate loans can be troublesome in the succession process because the owner often has pledged significant assets and negotiated favorable terms. But a successor without significant assets to pledge may be less attractive to a bank for long-term loans or renewal of a credit line during the transition. However, a banking institution works hard at acquiring new business due to the competitiveness of the financial marketplace. From a consulting prospective, an astute business owner can use the bank's services to evaluate a business plan and should expand that capability to the succession planning. From the bank's perspective, it should eagerly participate in all planning activities that add to client retention. A knowledgeable and supportive banker is one of the best professional relationships an owner can have.

- **Insurance Agent.** More often than not, an insurance agent seems motivated to assist in succession planning discussions for personal compensation issues. The industry as a whole has a reputation for being too transactional oriented and not focused on the long-term needs of the client. But an insurance agent may be a good referral source for the attorneys and other tax advisors that can address thorny issues in the transfer of a private business. An owner can secure a long-term relationship with this advisor when the agent's commitment to remain proactive on a timely basis is real. But I have found those situations are the exception not the rule with aggressive life insurance agents due to "heaped" front-end commissions.

- **Attorney.** A lawyer often has the technical expertise to interpret the law and provides excellent research and communication skills. But I have found that many business owners resist the legal profession in succession counseling due to the expense. Owners do not perceive value, and the temperaments of the two parties are different. Questions are often complex and warrant research. Due to the fast pace of the business world, the owner looks for answers immediately, and do not have the time to wait for detailed legal opinions for daily operations or succession planning. Finally, most attorneys want to hold meetings in their offices. This means the owner has to go through the hassle of traveling to the meeting as well as taking time away from running the business. For some owners, the best option is to establish a succession plan and then send it to an attorney for review just prior to execution.

- **Family Counselor.** Believe it or not, a therapist can often be an important resource for the owner to use in the succession planning process. Stress occurs due to poor parent-child relations or various psychological disorders that often develop in a family company when the commitment to the business is greater than prompt resolution of family issues. Wealth generated by a successful business may also lead to emotional trauma that needs professional assistance. Some trained therapists have a unique skill set for developing communication between parties and can be a great asset to multi-generational family business. Retreats for the family, board of directors, or management workshops facilitated by an appropriately trained therapist can be highly effective and defuse conflicts during the succession planning process.

- **Bank Trust Officer.** The duties of a trust officer to the beneficiaries of the trust can, at times, be difficult. When a grantor designs the trust, the need for an institutional successor trustee is often recommended by the lawyer. In my experience, the grantor often does not fully comprehend the long-term implications of the authority that will be granted to the successor trustee. The bank trustee is then left to interpret the words of the document and act accordingly. My recommendation is that the trust officer should be excluded from the succession planning process because of a potential conflict of interest.

Attitude is everything in succession planning, and the following story illustrates how simple and effective the process can be if all parties are open to building a better future.

After I recently presented the 7 Steps to Succession℠ at a contractor's annual convention in Florida, I was approached by a few of the attendees. An elderly gentleman, who introduced himself as Joe, said, "Nice presentation, I have already completed my succession plan."

I responded, "How did you do it?

He said, "I e mailed my family that I was going to get out, and wrote if anyone was interested, they should respond!"

His son-in-law, who I had met earlier in the day, stood nearby and confirmed the facts. The younger man joined the conversation to elaborate on the situation. I quickly learned how four of the siblings had come together with the son-in-law to take over the company. This, of course, fascinated me. Later, when I returned to Chicago, I contacted Joe at his northern Indiana office to find out if he would be interested in sharing his succession planning story with me, and he agreed.

One of Joe's sons, who had been briefed about my mission, greeted me when I arrived at the company headquarters on the day of the meeting. As I entered the main office, Joe had a big grin on his face and warmly shook my hand. Then he introduced me to one of his daughters, and I then spotted his son-in-law, who had become president of the company. He graciously accepted my greeting and welcomed me to the firm. Joe apologized about the absence of his other son, who was at home with his wife and just-born grandchild.

For the next several hours, Joe gave me a detailed history of the company dating back to the 1960s and told me about his immediate family. We continued our discussion with me asking him to describe the e-mail about selling the company. He explained he and his wife had sent a simple message from their home computer four years ago. Although he didn't have a hard copy of it, it was easy enough for him to recall the contents. It read:

TO: Children (4) and in-laws (2)

FROM: Dad and Mom

SUBJECT: Company for sale; cheap

Anyone interested in becoming an owner, contact the undersigned.

Joe and Jane

All recipients replied immediately!

We continued our discussion of the facts leading up to the e-mail. Briefly, a key employee had been given the opportunity to enter into discussions about buying the company. But a deal couldn't be worked out, and the key employee left the business. Nonetheless, Joe and his wife discussed their retirement plans with the hope of letting go of the business by the time Joe was 65.

I asked Joe how he did his research about succession planning. He explained he had an excellent local attorney and his wife had been working as a secretary in a CPA's office. She brought home articles on business valuation and stock transfer techniques to children.

The couple identified several key issues: Valuation of the business, gifting of the stock, the buy sell agreement, long-term lease for the building in which the business was located (still owned by Joe and his wife in a trust), and company policy about children (and grandchildren) needing to work outside the firm before joining the family business.

I kept listening for a key issue that was not resolved but didn't find one. Joe explained that he had insisted that the children work out the details of the succession plan and described a meeting in the local bank's board room where the new successors spent several hours sorting out job responsibilities and ownership formulas. It seemed the major steps had been taken, and Joe was satisfied he could let go.

They then sought the counsel of the attorney, and a succession plan was quickly crafted and executed. The last gift of stock, with a 30% minority interest discount, had been completed in December of the prior year.

Joe was still an employee, only with a smaller office. When he came to work on January 2nd of next year, he met is oldest son as he entered the building.

Joe asked him, "What do you want me to do?"

His son replied, "Carry on."

CHAPTER FOUR:

DISCOVERY AND COMMITMENT

The second phase of the 7 Steps to Succession[SM] in The McCabe Arch involves discovery and valuation of all assets in the founder's portfolio and then challenges the commitment of both the founder and the successor to the planning process.

Simply put, this is where all parties become aware of the financial ramifications and feasibility of a transfer in ownership of the company. Both generations and their advisors must actively participate during this stage of the process to demonstrate a will to succeed.

Economic Review
- Determination if projected assets are sufficient to support lifestyle.

- Preliminary valuation of business value.

Formal Education
- Credentials to demonstrate competence & specialization BBA and industry training.

- Complete an employment assignment outside of the family firm.

CPA & Mentor

2

1

2

1

Founder

Successor

Copyright ©2004 Harry M. McCabe
All rights reserved

For the founder, the most important component of the discovery phase is a detailed economic review, which utilizes a fact finder that has been developed to give a snapshot of net worth. The fact finder categorizes different asset classes, and a dollar value is given to each asset class. If the asset, for instance, is a husband's individual retirement account (IRA), then the most current value of the IRA is listed. We search for as much detail as possible at this point to identify the net worth of the founder as well as the spouse. Secondarily, we must determine how the assets are titled in order to establish potential gift strategies and eventual estate distributions. This plan is done with a CPA's assistance to calculate income, inheritance, and estate tax implications.

The discovery process also is an important tool that helps the senior generation take stock of their true goals and objectives. They must ask themselves:

> How much money is enough in retirement?
> When do they want their children to control significant wealth?

The private business, with its capacity to generate income, might be one of the most valuable assets to the family. During the economic review, we also need to determine if current managers, including the successor, adhere and promote the core values mentioned in earlier chapters.

But self-discovery is often difficult, especially for owners trying to quantify their net worth. I often find a lack of commitment to the succession plan process whenever the owner fails to complete the fact finder worksheets. In these cases, the process should be halted in order to save the owner and successor time, energy, emotional distress about passing the torch, and fees related to the succession planning process.

I purposefully stretch the timeline during the economic review and force the founder to focus on the financial aspects of succession planning over a long period of time instead of making decisions too quickly. As part of my pension consulting background, I often worked with individuals approaching retirement in a similar manner. My numerical analysis of their particular situation always included projections of income needed to support their lifestyle during retirement. These estimates openly challenged retirees to answer questions about the cash flow needed to support them without earned income.

Addressing this issue typically leads to detailed conversations about travel and leisure activities. This can be a sensitive area because it involves lifelong dreams of places to go and things to do that retirees never did during their active working lives. Open discussions about where they want to eventually reside sometimes spur contradictory and difficult responses. A spouse once described her dream retirement location as a house on a golf course in Arizona while her husband spoke about living near his coveted fishing boat anchored in South Florida.

After completing the fact finder, the owner and spouse jointly review the forms with me. I start to question them about the various asset holdings. The meetings can take a humorous tone. For instance, a trust may have been established, funded and controlled by a one parent. When the *real* dollar amount is put on the form, the spouse is often surprised and provides me with an insight to the level of communication that exists between the couple at the financial level.

Commonly, we find either the husband or wife has secretly put an extra stash of money aside, just in case of an emergency. Other times, the couple just forgets that they have a long-term CD, stock, or bond. These are what I call "quiet assets," which are locked away in a safe or bank safety deposit box and don't generate a lot of activity.

My role is to get *all* assets accounted for so that we can do meaningful projections and determine the level of income surplus or shortfall that might be reasonably expected. With the help of a CPA and other financial advisors, we then determine the tax basis of these assets and put them on the shelf for later consideration.

By putting our numbers into financial planning software, we can collaboratively develop calculations to help determine different cash flow scenarios, utilizing contributions to and withdrawals from the asset pool as well as asset growth rates, inflation, and income tax rates.

The calculations also take into account an estimate of Social Security benefits upon retirement. When the reports are generated and reviewed, I search for the reactions from the owner and spouse. They can range from "Is that all I've got?" to "Why am I still working?"

I often run these calculations with a minimum value attached to the business because the goal for many owners in the discovery process is to determine if there are sufficient assets to support a comfortable lifestyle and still give the business away to a worthy internal successor. Determining income flow over a long period of time astounds people. When you think about the percentage of disposable income used in their retirement years for medical expenses and apply a double-digit inflation rate to those services, the total amount of money devoted to the necessities of life creates an uncomfortable stir amongst most retirees.

Since my fact finder is also designed to determine who has ownership of property, part of the discussion at this second stage involves eventual distribution of the property at the demise of the parties. The needs of a special child or grandchildren as well as extraordinary bequeaths to other family members and philanthropic interests may have been already designed in a will or special trust, so I review these documents. At times, this block has already been assembled, and we can refine the provisions later in the seven-step process.

It is nice to dream about retirement from a private business, but the reality of the situation is that the G-2 owner needs to be developed. When you think about the different stages of family life, the education of a child is often a long-term goal established when the infant is born. For example, I attended my first prenatal class with my wife at a hospital, where a nurse prepared young couples for parenthood. First, she addressed the physical changes that women would go through. Then the nurse shocked me when she looked at the group and asked. "What's the biggest concern husbands have?"

She wrote "MONEY" on the chalkboard. For me, she hit the nail right on the head. An expanding family meant my wife would not work, and we would lose her earning power. How was I going to pay for the pending hospital bill over the short-term let alone ever-growing college tuition eighteen years later? The nurse sure got each man in the room thinking about the future and how to pay for it.

In a family business scenario, the senior generation typically has cleared the hurdle of general education expenses for their offspring and has focused on preparing for the next major challenge of financial independence: retirement. However, the successor generation may need development of specific skills before taking control, and a parent is still a parent and must aid in the continuing education of a successor.

So let's turn to the successor side of the arch. Formal education should now be complete, with a bachelor's degree (or equivalent) and even a master's degree. Advanced studies in a chosen field should always be undertaken for continuing education. It's my theory that an undergraduate degree demonstrates a capacity for learning, and an advanced degree indicates specific knowledge. Ideally, general and specific fields of knowledge can to be applied in the working environment of a family business.

A basic, four-year degree is a must. It provides some credibility, but the debate still rages as to the practicality of many formal academic components. College frequently does not develop leadership or creative thinking skills nor promote the entrepreneurial spirit of students.

It is well documented that the second generation often lends a hand in the family business while growing up. Sometimes it's economic necessity because the parents can't afford to pay day care expenses or hire employees. But working in a family business also exposes the second generation to the inner workings of a business so that they learn firsthand many of the techniques and terminology intrinsic to the business.

But I sometimes think parents expect a child to learn the business by osmosis. My first work experience was at a startup restaurant on Chicago's Southside that my Dad had a small economic interest in. Together with the managing partner's son, we were the first official dishwashers. I was underage, but my Dad thought the experience would be good for me.

My newfound friend Randy didn't particularly like to work for his father, the general manager. We both directly reported to the head chef, who was in charge of the kitchen. Our numerous assignments included peeling potatoes and preparing other food as well as scrubbing pots and pans and cleaning up the food preparation areas. This meant everything from mopping floors and scrubbing the meat chopping block with a steel brush to tossing out the garbage. Then the dinner plates, glassware, and silverware were cleaned, sanitized, and stored for the next day. I learned firsthand the workflow of a professional kitchen and was proud to have earned my first paycheck. Then I received a promotion to salad preparer and didn't have to wash dishes, which became my first lesson in career advancement.

Other lessons came later in life when I worked for a different family business in suburban Chicago and observed how sibling rivalry, birth order, and gender impact the future generation of leadership in a company. These are important issues for anyone who even thinks about working in a family business.

Once the second generation completes a formal college education program, I firmly recommend that the individual find a job outside the family business. The proficiency and knowledge that can be attained through outside employment can prove to be very valuable if the individual returns to the family business at a later date. Formal training programs may exist at larger employers that simply cannot be funded at smaller private companies. For instance, marketing and sales training techniques for some products and services may be easily adapted to the family business.

Likewise, financial accounting, database management, human resource training, and research and development management at outside companies can provide valuable work experience for the successor generation. Leadership training and competition against peers can also be valuable experience second-generation successors can bring back to their family businesses.

Most importantly, the achievements and awards earned by the second-generation in another work environment can be helpful in alleviating the perception of nepotism in the family business. Co-workers see adults with diplomas and achievement plaques on the office wall and evaluate for themselves the skill of the successor for future management and leadership.

The key employee group may have previously seen the child in the workplace. However, they may now compete with the second-generation for management positions, better salaries, and advancement opportunities. They may sense the preferential treatment provided to the family member and might even feel discriminated against. These unhealthy perceptions can be detrimental to the long-term success of the business enterprise. But all that can be avoided with thoughtful planning. An example:

When Julie Copeland, a third-generation CEO and president of Philadelphia-based Arbill Safety, joined the family company, there was no guarantee that her father would pass the business down to her. "There were several things I did to prepare that I would recommend to any potential successor," she writes in *Family Business* magazine.

Copeland lists the steps she took to demonstrate to her father, her fellow employees, and her customers that she was qualified to become the company's next CEO and president:

> Obtain an MBA. "Doing so gave me the background in accounting and finance that I would later need as a business leader. It also gave me confidence. I started to realize that if I could complete projects and achieve high grades in business school, I could succeed in the business world."

> Set goals. "I compiled a three-page list of goals that I wanted to fulfill prior to becoming president. For example, I set out to improve my understanding of bank relations and financial management. Doing so enabled me to demonstrate to my father that I was serious about taking over and capable of setting and meeting goals."

> Join a support/networking group. "I joined a support group that was instrumental in coaching me through the transition by helping me plan and manage emotional issues."

> Realize early on that you have the capability to change. "The transition becomes easier if you realize that you are the one who can adjust, adapt, and change. Recognizing and respecting the fact that your senior-generation relative likely has been in business for as long as you've been alive and probably has an established way of doing things can go a long way toward helping you work together and cooperate."

In the succession planning process, mentoring the next generation becomes just plain, old-fashioned common sense. The literature is mixed on when and how to implement a formal mentoring program, and it often "depends on the situation."

My general recommendations:

• Continue formal education programs and obtain industry specific certifications, licenses, and credentials;

- Establish reasonable, attainable goals determined jointly by the supervisor and successor;

- Find leadership advancement opportunities outside the business in civic, political, and social organizations;

- Join industry-oriented study groups to develop peer-to-peer relations and look for additional mentoring opportunities;

- Widen the scope of a career path and constantly raise the bar for performance and accountability. A personal development scorecard will prove to be a valuable building block.

Overall, the path to self-discovery and commitment by all parties must be evaluated at this point in the 7 Steps to Succession℠ process. If the owner demands that a designated successor participate in the process and the individual just goes through the motions, the process—and perhaps the future of the company—may be doomed. There must be a real fire in the belly of the designated successor to assume ownership and leadership of the company.

At the conclusion of the second phase, there must be momentum for both owner and successor to search for the key issues that will need to be resolved to complete the succession plan.

CHAPTER FIVE:

ORDERLY TRANSFER

Passing the baton in a track relay race symbolizes the completion of one leg of the event with the simultaneous beginning of another by a different runner. However, a smooth handoff takes place only after many hours of practice so that both parties in the exchange are comfortable with the motion and feel of the transaction. That's precisely what happens in the third phase of 7 Steps to Succession[SM].

This step involves transferring key elements of the company's economics from the owner to the successor, including client relationships, referral sources, and vendor and key supplier relationships. To help the owner think about this critical activity and organize his thoughts about the inner workings of the business and trade secrets, I require him to assemble a special marketing plan.

Marketing Plan
- Orderly transfer of clients.

- Introduction to existing vendors and product providers.

Build Client Base
- Specialization & core competencies emerge.

- Complete assignments.

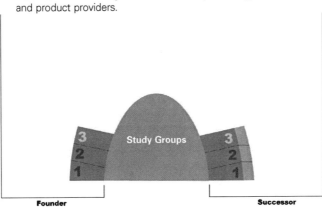

Copyright ©2004 Harry M. McCabe
All rights reserved

I ask that the plan be written, so that successor and appropriate advisors can study and understand what brings revenue into the front door of the business. After all, without top line revenue there may not have a sustainable business to pass on. I often find that successful entrepreneurs keep an eye on different benchmarks, depending on the business, but *all* owners keep an eye on the cash flow generated from various sales activities.

Quite naturally, the G-1 owner hesitates to turn over his top clients to the younger generation. Why? The top tier, known as "A" clients, provides significant revenue to the firm, has great upside potential, offers a window to other business opportunities, and may have taken years to develop. The owner fears that a transfer of this valuable relationship to someone else will disturb the client. As I've been told by numerous owners. "I've worked too hard to gain this account to let my immature son destroy it!"

Extending the firm's existing marketing niche to fit the G-2's natural abilities will increase the likelihood of sustaining the profitability of the venture. The successor must demonstrate a proficiency to grow the business one way or another.

In reality, the successor must develop a client base, referral sources, and centers of influence when in a sales position. An area of specialization will begin to emerge. It can be product specific, whereby proper research and due diligence has been done on a product line not currently offered by the business. After a successful test market, the owner may be more receptive to introducing the successor to his top clients, but the successor must be given the chance to test his mettle because he must find ways to complement the founder, not be a clone.

However, a skillful family can promote the entrepreneurial spirit of its younger generation by allocating certain venture capital to be used for experimental projects. This research and development function can be maintained in the existing business or spun out into new entities with various shared ownership structures.

By utilizing the capabilities of successful new ventures to enhance marketing efforts, client acquisition, and cross-selling opportunities to existing clients, we often find that the objectives of orderly transfer get accomplished.

Generally, the owner is asked to take another leap of faith at this point during the orderly transfer phase with in-depth discussions about company secrets and competitive weaknesses. These discussions are about trust, which includes the owner coming clean about the financial viability of the company.

What the owner fails to realize, though, is that the successor probably figured out most of economics and marketing plan because the individual has assembled bits and pieces of it during previous internal job assignments. This awareness can create awkward moments, and the owner often quietly says, "I didn't know you knew that." That's when I know there is mutual respect and trust, which is a good indicator that the succession plan will be completed.

It also is important for the owner and successor to discuss "B" and "C" clients that range from mid-to-low or no profitability. One topic in this area always creates an interesting exchange among the generations: loss leaders. Essentially, this method involves selling a product at or below a breakeven price to get in the door of a client with the hopes of later providing higher profit margin products and services. But too many loss leaders turn out to be a drain on time and resources, which amount to a net financial loss, and never provide a second opportunity to sell other products to make up revenue.

The owner should limit exposure to loss leaders and "C" clients because the company cannot sustain itself with only that sales technique. I also advise an owner to limit the number of "C" clients given to the successor to avoid the frustration of dealing with minor players who will not contribute to the financial well being of the company.

Overall, success of the business may well depend on building many long-term profitable client relationships, which is beneficial to the owner and successor because one of the natural advantages of a private company is passing the client base from one generation to the next.

In addition to client segmentation and ranking, the owner should include other **critical** components in the special marketing plan:

- Gross revenue targets;
- Description of product and services;
- Specific sales techniques;
- Advantages over competitors;
- Development of brand loyalty;
- Advertising.

The responsibility to prioritize major marketing initiatives should be followed by written details to coordinate with the entire budget, administration of events, and programs with external parties.

At this point, it is prudent for all parties to consider the strengths of the successor. Perhaps the second-generation has developed a proficiency in technology that can be applied to the business. I have often seen the need for a new web site to better market products, new accounting systems to provide more accurate financial data, and relational contact management programs. The skills of G-2, who grew up with computers in every aspect of their life, may be better suited to bring this value-added technology to a family-run business.

I also encourage G-2 to extend technology efficiencies to the customer. The increased visibility gained by the successor should add depth to the client relationship, but technology initiatives need to be measured for both company and the client to maximize impact and demonstrate success.

The marketing plan can be revised during this phase of 7 Steps to Succession℠ by introducing the successor to higher-level projects with more responsibility and financial importance. This practice needs to be repeated for a successful and orderly transfer of the company similar to runners circling a track. The reason is simple: Cross pollinating both generations will build mutual respect, trust, and humility and set the stage for new growth and success.

Through cross-pollination, G-2 gains more and more confidence about leading the company in the future. For example, one successor related one of the few success stories I've ever heard about "C" clients. He had been assigned three-dozen with the goal of turning the clients into profitable relationships within ten months or terminating them. The protégé, using his entrepreneurial risk-taking personality, devised an *exclusive* sale price for one product with favorable payment terms and a series of breakpoints in pricing based on size of the order.

The timing for the incentives turned out to be perfect. Eleven clients bought the product incentive plan and moved up to "B" status based on sales volume plus tie-in product sales, and the protégé terminated relationships with the other twenty-five. Moral of the story: By openly setting congruent goals, the company and the successor achieved victory.

Over the years, I also worked with many successful multi-generational construction companies. Their measurement techniques are different for client retention—and almost everything else—because once a construction project is complete the relationship is often over, but a need to measure performance still exists. For instance, one client gave me a quizzical look when I asked how business was going. He explained that they were busier than ever and then produced hand-written tabular notes, which tracked the number of men working in the field. The owner said that he pulled these figures from accounting files because he wanted to accurately count the number of people working on all construction sites. Then he dug further in his desk drawer and produced similar papers stapled together. I examined the tattered and yellowed papers that covered two decades of data. This successful business owner kept the pulse of his business and compared current activities to historic data by extracting specific information from complicated payroll records and labor union reports, distilling it into a meaningful tracking system.

Another client, a road builder, explained that the paving season came to an end every year at the onset of winter because that was when asphalt plants closed. Consequently, she measured success by truckloads of asphalt, and "all I try to do is get as much asphalt on the ground as possible."

I often run into firm resistance from companies about changing anything about operations because current procedures work just fine. This culture must be recognized during the orderly transfer of client relations between generations. As the saying goes, "If it ain't broke, don't fix it." I have found family businesses in their second to third-generation transfer with some of these characteristics.

Peter Leach, a partner at accounting firm BDO Stoy Hayward and chairman of BDO Centre for Family Business, thinks one of the failings of many firms is their resistance to change. "Family businesses can be very introverted and don't want to look at what's really going on," he says. "Hard truths can get buried and there is a risk of becoming insular and complacent."

As an example, a multi-generational firm with two founders ran a lucrative specialty manufacturing plant in a western suburb of Chicago. The two owners later formed a partnership outside the business to purchase the building and land from which the business operated. The firm's founders each had one son working in the business.

Upon the death of one founder, the surviving founder bought full ownership of the building and land while the son of the decedent inherited half of the business. Rent payments to the surviving partner at market value were fixed for a ten-year term. When the second founder died, his wife inherited the property, and his son owned fifty percent of the business.

This co-owner insisted rent payments continue to be made to his mother at the same rate on renewal of the lease for another ten-year term. The profitability of the business had declined, and the rent payment amount became a hotly contested debate. The relationship of G-2 became stormy because they resisted change and could not work together, resulting in a bitter legal battle over control of the company.

In another situation, I observed a second-generation owner of a custom wood products company in a heated debate on the telephone over the price of wood per linear foot with a key vendor. Negotiations ended when my client explained that he would have to go to a competitive supplier. Then he slammed down the phone, his face red and his hands shaking with anger. When he settled down, the owner looked up at me from his desk, smiled, and said, "He'll call back in a few moments. This goes on every year."

Sure enough, the phone rang a few minutes later, and my client cordially negotiated a lower cost per linear foot. It took five minutes to close the deal.

"That's how you make money in this business," the owner happily said.

But a discussion of orderly transfer would not be complete without stressing the long-term nature of some products and services that are provided to clients. When I was in the pension business, I occasionally got a concerned look from the founder of a company.

"Who is going to be here to complete the plan?" the founder demanded.

I confidently explained the depth of my organization, which included my youngest brother. Similarly, both my cousin Tim and I were brought into the client relationships by Uncle George to help him answer that question for his "A" clients.

Uncle George (left) and Harry present a financial plan to a client as captured for Provident Life and Accident Insurance Company's 1980 Annual Report.

Overall, a family business must consider the balance between the growth of the client base through innovation versus what worked in the past, which challenges both G-1 and G-2 during the orderly transfer phase. This is where both generations must also reach out for more information and support provided by various study groups on multi-generational issues.

Academic institutions provide resources through research projects and family business workshops. In many metropolitan areas, industry and academia jointly sponsor these ventures. Professional organizations also provide educational substance on topics of ownership and management responsibilities as well as forums on other issues related to private business ownership. Peer groups, where intimacy and privacy are respected, provide a format to openly discuss new ideas with contemporaries.

Industry meetings have historically provided an excellent forum for private business owners to discuss sensitive issues with their friends in a golf cart during a leisurely eighteen-hole round. In some situations, a cocktail reception provides the best atmosphere to candidly discuss succession and transition issues.

The use of an organizational chart, with its visual representation, can be very effective for the owner and successor to understand the business that is to be passed on. Each box in the chart should contain the responsibilities and tasks of the specific manager and supporting team. Overlapping areas of responsibility can be identified, and the management team can make sure that everything is accounted for, so nothing falls through the cracks. As with any management tool, it should be periodically reviewed and updated to reflect changes in personnel or the business environment.

An additional management tool commonly used is an exercise known as a SWOT analysis (strengths, weaknesses, opportunities and threats). The exercise stimulates thinking about the organization and its internal capabilities as well as the external environment. The leadership team can combine an organizational chart with a SWOT exercise to identify both G-1 and G-2's current and future roles. By combining the organization's natural strengths with potential weaknesses, adjustments to a company's chain of command can be properly addressed.

In many of my consulting assignments, I invert the organizational chart diagram to turn it upside down. The various support functions of marketing, finance, information technology, research and development, and human resources must, after all, support the operations of the business that produce the goods and services. Each support area should look for efficiencies that contribute to the core profit centers of the enterprise.

In the inverted organizational wire diagram, the Board of Directors box is now at the bottom supporting the business. Ownership and management reach upward to identify the important tactical issues related to running the company during the ownership transfer to the successor.

A smooth handoff of the baton from one generation to another is the ultimate goal. Similar to runners in a track relay race, there can be multiple handoffs between G-1 and G-2 before the company completes its race. If, however, the baton is dropped during an exchange, the company doesn't lose the race. The owner and successor simply pick up the baton, make adjustments, and get back into the race.

Mistakes will be made, but commitment and good communication between G-1 and G-2 will allow anger and disappointment to subside and forgiveness and healing to occur during this emotional process.

The key to a successful plan is to begin early and not give up after dropping the baton.

CHAPTER SIX:

CRISIS PLAN

Events outside the control of the owner or successor normally cause disorderly transfers in a private business, and the fourth phase of the 7 Steps to Succession^{SM} addresses how contingency planning can minimize the trauma of unexpected events.

Although it is impossible to plan for every potential crisis, the owner and successor must jointly think about the unthinkable and inevitable: death of either party, long-term disability due to illness or accident, and events that can impact the operational and financial viability of the company.

Crisis Plan
- Written plan for Death and Disability of senior owner.
- Risk management.

Crisis Plan
- Commitment to honor terms of Buy/Sell agreement.
- Provide reciprocal provisions.

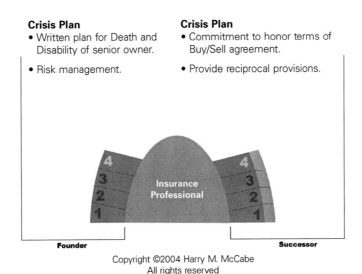

Founder

Insurance Professional

Successor

Copyright ©2004 Harry M. McCabe
All rights reserved

This requires the owner and successor to cement their commitment to each other and the business to make sure the company survives a crisis. By doing so, they guarantee their dedication to the firm, and their contractual agreement to each other will increase the probability that stakeholders will be properly rewarded.

Simply put, the owner needs to plan for sudden death or debilitating illness that will sideline him from the business while the successor needs to put "skin in the game" to financially demonstrate his commitment to be the next leader of the firm. It's put up or shut up time for both parties, and each should now understand that no one would be around forever.

There are two common types of a buy/sell agreement that provide for the continuity of a business. Both discourage owners and family shareholders, through the legal mechanism called the right of first refusal, from selling the company to an outside party if an owner dies, becomes disabled, or leaves the company for other reasons.

The first is known as an entity purchase agreement. As the name implies, this agreement is between the company and the shareholders. To fund the purchase, a business secures life insurance contracts insuring both owner and successor, and it pays the premiums. Therefore, the life insurance policies become company assets. The cash value of the policy can be paid to the insured stockholder for the redemption of stock if the individual leaves the company for retirement, disability, or any other reason. Upon the premature death of a majority shareholder, the business interest passes to the estate/heirs of the owner while the life insurance company pays the face amount to the business.

Then the deceased owner's estate/heirs sell their interest in the business back to the company under the terms of the buy/sell agreement. The business pays cash from the insurance policy to the estate/heirs for control of the company.

A second way to provide continuity is a cross purchase agreement between the shareholders. Each shareholder procures a life insurance policy insuring the life of the other shareholder. For example,

G-1 would be the policy owner, pay the premiums, and be the primary beneficiary of the life insurance policy insuring the life of G-2. Conversely, G-2 would buy a policy on the life of G-1 with full ownership rights and responsibility to pay the premium. Upon the untimely death of G-1, the policy face value would be paid to G-2, who would be obligated by the buy/sell agreement to purchase the decedent's interest in the business from G-1's estate.

Either type of buy/sell plan assures the family of a fair price and affords them timely access to the financial resources they may need for continued financial support. An orderly replacement of the departing owner preserves the direction, goals, and vision of the business as well as management harmony.

But the design of the buy/sell agreement is dependent on the structure of the company, tax implications, and administrative concerns. For instance, a cross-purchase plan works nicely with a two-shareholder scenario, and the remaining shareholder will often have a higher tax basis for the repurchased decedent's stock that could result in favorable tax treatment in the future sale of the business.

I lean toward an entity purchase agreement if there are numerous shareholders because fewer insurance policies need to be issued and accounted for.

From a personal perspective, I can attest to the success of the buy/sell agreement because of the planning that my father and uncle did at Consolidated Pension Consultants, Inc. They entered into an entity purchase type agreement. Both my uncle and father signed the agreement as individuals as well as officers of the company. The company funded the plan with life insurance, meaning the policy was paid for and owned by the company. The company was also the primary beneficiary of the face amount. Under the terms of my Dad's Last Will and Testament, my mother inherited the one hundred shares that represented his fifty percent stake in the business.

The buy/sell agreement called for CPC to buy her inherited one hundred shares at the stated value, and the life insurance proceeds provided the liquidity to complete my father's wishes. While Uncle George continued to own and grow the business, the cash from the purchase of my Dad's one hundred shares helped fund an estate-planning program, which included the establishment of a trust to provide for the needs of my mother and the future education of my younger siblings.

I'm very grateful of the fact that Dad and Uncle George planned and completed a succession agreement that covered all bases. Upon my father's premature death, Uncle George kept his outstanding one hundred shares, which gave him full control of CPC. As an owner with one hundred percent control, he continued to develop the business. My mother was financially sound and comfortably raised my two younger brothers and sister. Some of their living expenses and college education were partly funded from this bypass trust fund.

∞ ∞ ∞ ∞

As part of my work with family companies, I also include contingency planning exercises during the fourth phase of the succession planning process. These exercises probe important but overlooked aspects of the business.

Termination of employment at or prior to normal retirement should also be addressed by asking the question, Will the business allow non-working owners?

For example, the valuation of the business often becomes outdated and must be reviewed and perhaps recalculated every few years to keep up with inflation and profitability because valuation inaccuracies lead to complications and misunderstandings among survivors and their advisors.

Sometimes I find that a company's crisis plan lacks depth and fails to cover all transfer events and what happens in the event of sale or transfer to a third-party or involuntary ownership transfer due to bankruptcy or divorce.

Ironically, insurance coverage can be problematic. For instance, changes in the percentage of stock held by a person may occur during the transition of ownership and may cause a shift in the amount of coverage for each shareholder.

Additionally, it is critical to double-check that beneficiary designations are in line with the actual buy/sell agreement. Through a lack of proper documentation, it is possible for heirs to receive the face amount of the insurance policy *and* inherit the ownership interest of the deceased.

∞ ∞ ∞ ∞

Both the owner and the successor must also protect the business through proper risk management techniques to guard against personal or professional loss that could destroy the company and leave nothing to pass on to heirs or successors.

Did you, as a parent, ever get a phone call that woke you from a sound sleep at two o'clock in the morning? A friend of mine did after his son, a sophomore in college, had borrowed his car for the evening to visit friends. His son was not severely injured in the car accident, but the student's reckless driving caused the fatality of an innocent bystander. What followed was a long, ugly, and grueling lawsuit that resulted in significant payments from family assets for restitution.

This story clearly illustrates the need to develop a contingency plan for wealth preservation of a family business that includes asset protection strategies. A risk management review should include potential liability of:

- Lawsuits from:
    - Accidents with damages, physical injuries, and death;
    - Psychological trauma;
    - Malpractice;
    - Negligence;
    - Fraud and Misrepresentation;
- Business Setbacks, (i.e. creditors);
- Divorce.

How do you protect yourself? Liability insurance, even in uncertain markets with tighter underwriting standards, must be considered the first line of defense. But please remember liability insurance is not a cure-all since carriers change availability of coverage in risky areas and do not hesitate to raise rates at renewal.

The legal structure of the company may prove helpful but can be vulnerable to attacks from aggressive attorneys who try to pierce corporate or LLC structures on a procedural basis to get to family wealth. In extreme cases, declaring bankruptcy will provide some relief, but the Bankruptcy Abuse Prevention and Consumer Protection Act of 2005 has made this option less desirable since many provisions now favor creditors.

A solid asset protection strategy can be implemented by obtaining adequate liability insurance and optimizing exempt assets. Then consider rules governing trusts and corporations in other states as well as their judicial system. Finally, give some consideration to moving some assets offshore as a last safe haven but always get expert opinion from your financial advisors and attorneys to make sure that everything is legal and compliant.

It really pays to be prepared for any contingency that could shut down your business. I, for example, went to my office early one Monday morning when I owned Retirement Programs Corporation in Burr Ridge, Illinois. After walking through the vestibule of the office building, I approached my office door to discover that the lock had been pried open.

I cautiously opened the door to enter my office suite, walked down the main aisle between the workstations, and instantly felt something was wrong. Then I noticed a computer monitor ajar near the reception desk and quickly looked under the desk to discover that the personal computer was missing. I glanced across the room and found other workstations in disarray, moved to where we stored our data backup tapes, popped the backup disk out of the machine, and slipped it into my pocket.

Then I discovered other PCs, a VCR, fax machine, and other office equipment had been stolen. My heart sunk as I called 911 to get the police. Ironically, their office was located less than a half a block away. Numerous thoughts raced through my mind during this crisis. How much damage was really done to the business? What would it cost to replace all the equipment? Did we lose irreplaceable information?

I was somewhat comforted by the fact that this incident had occurred over the weekend and none of my employees were injured or put in jeopardy. Yet I had a sickening feeling in my stomach that I had been victimized by robbery.

A few hours later, the police completed their preliminary investigation, but a sergeant told me that the robbers had probably disposed of my equipment within hours of the break-in. Fortunately, my brother Mike and I found one workstation still intact and determined that our backup system had worked and our data was secure. As the day progressed, a technology consultant gave me the replacement cost for the office equipment, computers, monitors, printers, and fax machines. Then I contacted the insurance company in mid-afternoon to verify my coverage and report my claim while I simultaneously reviewed the riders to the policies.

By four that afternoon, my IT expert walked into a big-box computer warehouse ready to purchase a few replacement items, but I put her on hold to complete a conversation with the insurance agent who explained that I had business interruption riders that would cover replacement cost for all of the missing items. I got back on the line with the IT expert and said, "Buy everything you need, and let's get it installed tonight."

Later that evening, I sat in my office exhausted but believed we had been lucky. It would take only two days to get up and running again after the new equipment was installed. I knew we'd never catch the thieves, but I felt good about my management of the crisis. The company had been prepared for this kind of traumatic event by installing a backup data system and buying the right insurance, which made me feel like a darn good manager. My last decision of the day was to install a better security deadbolt system for the new front door as soon as possible to avoid a future intrusion. The loss of a few electronic items is nothing. What if your business was destroyed by fire or flood?

Believe it or not, the owner or successor of private company should also make a contingency plan that covers divorce because going through one can be personally agonizing and financially terrifying. I'm a case study on how to handle this kind of situation, so allow me to tell a brief story about how I titled several private stock holdings in a revocable living trust and caused additional anguish during the crisis of my divorce.

One day I found myself in the back of a courtroom in DuPage County, Illinois, observing my divorce attorney, opposing counsel, and a divorce judge discussing a petition brought by opposing counsel objecting to the way I had titled private stock in the living trust. The defining moment occurred when the judge asked, "Why would anyone title private stock in a revocable living trust?"

Both attorneys looked at each other in utter silence. They glanced at the judge but no one said a word. I stood up, raised my hand, and walked towards the front of the courtroom,

"Your honor," I said, "may I approach the bench?"

He responded rather forcefully. "Mr. McCabe, sit down, or I'll hold you in contempt of court."

I immediately fell into the first open chair I could find, and then the judge called a two-hour recess during which my lawyer explained that I should never do that again in court.

But I took advantage of the break and told my attorney that he needed to know more about why business owners use trusts to protect their privacy. When we reconvened, the judge cited other cases in which trusts and beneficiary arrangements had been used, and he dismissed the petition. He concluded his remarks by saying these financial instruments are appropriate estate planning tools.

He then looked me dead in the eye, nodded, struck his gavel, and said, "This court is adjourned."

I felt relieved and vindicated but also knew I had just wasted a day of my life in court and just spent a bundle on legal fees for the day. But the stock in the trust was proper and not subject to retitling as petitioned, so we could now get to the next item in the divorce proceeding.

The dissolution of a marriage can create many difficulties for family business owners. A prime example is when a G-2 owner inherits family wealth and co-mingles it with marital assets. Depending on the state of domicile, a disgruntled spouse may have a valid claim to shares of the family business.

∞   ∞   ∞   ∞

The lack of a crisis plan can create havoc at any company. A sad but true story illustrates the point. I recently placed a follow-up telephone call for an invitation that I mailed to Howard Young about an executive briefing on succession planning. The receptionist forwarded my call to a gentleman named Jim who quickly explained that Mr. Young had died three months earlier. After giving Jim my condolences, he bemoaned the fact that Mr. Young was 92 years old at the time of his death.

I continued our discussion by explaining the nature of my call and asked Jim if he was part of the new ownership. "No, I'm the sales manager," he said. Then I asked to speak to the new owner and Jim responded, "I would love to let you, but he is 86 years old and on a respirator!"

Pausing briefly to reflect on my invitation about getting successful business owners to think strategically about succession, Jim said, "I wish you had called a year ago."

I agreed and asked if there was a buy/sell agreement in place between the co-owners. "I don't know," he responded. "There may be a trust in place for the ailing gentleman. I guess the grandkids are going to end up owning this company." I wound up the conversation by asking if it would be okay to check back in forty-five days to see if I could meet with the Key Management Team to discuss planning techniques for them to consider.

Forty-five days later, I called him back. "Jim, thanks for taking my call. Could I arrange a meeting with you and the key employees to discuss your needs and potentially see if there is a fit for my consulting services?"

He responded, "Harry I would like to introduce you to my boss, but there are quite a few other people trying to get in here right now, including the banker!" Then he explained that he was extremely pressed for time and "we really do not know what's going to happen. But stay in touch. I have your contact information."

Each crisis discussed in this chapter can have a short or long-term impact on a business owner and successor and their ability to complete a succession plan. Some setbacks are temporary and can be easily overcome. Others, though, can derail a lifetime of work.

By thinking the unthinkable and planning for tragedy, you can vastly improve your ability to overcome the adversity that is inherent in today's society and business world.

FLEXIBILITY

After completing the first four phases of the 7 Steps to Succession^{SM}, we can easily make adjustments to the overall goals of the succession plan if the work that has been done thus far has led us to the conclusion that we should not be continuing down a specific path.

What would cause a dramatic course correction? It might be as simple as the designated successor declaring, "Let's sell the company because we all can make more money, and I don't have to run it long-term."

Or it may be the owner who realizes that more capital will be required to maintain a certain style of living in retirement or that health care costs during the Golden Years will be double or triple the original predictions. Therefore, the business must be sold to an outside party to create additional wealth and meet the requirements of the owner.

Any planning process that cannot adjust to the internal needs of the major players or external business conditions is doomed to fail. Competition in a free-market economy provides many surprises, and we must be nimble yet firm in our conviction to complete a multi-generational plan. A proper succession planning process requires a balance between achieving the original goals versus adaptability to new conditions. The situation really is no different than a sailor gently adjusting the rudder and trimming the sails for a different course to a new destination.

I encourage flexibility in planning throughout the seven-step process because business owners need to take advantage of every tool they can find in order to accomplish their mission. Remember statistics tell us that only thirty percent of family businesses succeed from the first generation to the second and an even more dismal twelve percent survive to generation three. It is quite feasible that a company whose owners planned for succession may change course and eventually sell the business to meet the needs of either G-1 or G-2.

If that is the case, a merger and acquisition team—which could include an investment banker, an intermediary, and a transaction attorney—might need to be assembled. The personalities and competencies of these experts must blend in with the existing team for efficiencies, which is no easy task. Company executives need to recognize this challenge and actively integrate various skill sets with team building exercises while resetting objectives and delegating new tasks to special advisors.

But what happens when consensus cannot be achieved and stalemates occur at numerous points in the planning process?

Although it takes extra work, I continually sort the issues and prioritize them to ascertain the highest in importance. The process seeks to build on the facts as they have been developed while updating assumptions about future developments. By its very nature, this type of planning process will overcome obstacles and will find compromises in the design solution to achieve flexibility.

However, there may be times when we must backtrack and adjust a particular building block in The McCabe Arch because we may have found an initial assumption to be inaccurate. For example, the owner changes the timeline for the eventual transition of authority and responsibility because he wants to stay active in management and ownership for a longer period of time. The support team needs to analyze the new development and make recommendations to the company's leaders so the proper adjustments can be made.

Perhaps gifting of stock or interests in a Family Limited

Partnership (FLP) should be suspended for a year or two. By taking a new financial snapshot and adjusting the transfer into a longer time horizon, we can present the results to the owner and successor for consideration. Persuasion, discussion, and eventual resolution will result in the approval of a new timeline for the plan.

On occasion, I need to be more flexible and realize that a member of the supporting cast may need to be changed. It could be due to time limitations, lack of knowledge in the subject area, or even a conflict of interest that will weaken the overall support mechanism for succession planning. As The McCabe Arch continues in its upward ascent, we might have inadvertently stretched the capabilities of advisors.

Occasionally, a member of the support team fears that he may lose a profitable client relationship when engaging in the succession or exit planning process. I personally experienced this emotion while working for privately held business owners as their pension consultant. In conjunction with a CPA, attorney, banker, insurance agent, and another advisor, we helped the business owner develop a profitable business, which eventually provided the owner with handsome rewards when he sold. The buyer had his own pension plan administrator, and I found myself losing the client.

The same thing occurred in a planning engagement because the next generation perceived me as his Dad's consultant/advisor and wanted to bring in his own team. Thus, I lost the client by doing my job properly.

This dilemma continues to exist for most support teams in various relationships. I believe it causes hidden resistance to the planning process. A trusted advisor who wants to keep a long-term friendship and business relationship with the owner often thwarts collaboration with others. Withholding valuable information, not attending meetings, or delaying the planning process under the guise of obtaining more research or expert opinion is easily done by an advisor bent on complicating the transfer of the company.

At other times, all parties need to be flexible and open to ideas that might benefit the company's bottom line before or after succession. For instance, I recently worked with a third-generation family business when an unexpected development appeared in the form of a new business opportunity that one member of G-3 perceived to be most urgent. The information surfaced during a review meeting of the research and development team, and the concept was immediately fast-tracked to senior management for consideration.

Then the proposal was sent to appropriate decision makers and advisors with instructions to convene via conference call within a week. Since we had already established open communication lines with the principal parties, preparation for the conference call was minimal. The special advisors quickly and thoroughly evaluated the concept during the call, and the company's executive team pushed for a vote to resolve the matter. Although the new business opportunity was rejected, management concluded the call with positive recognition of the third generation's effort.

In fact, top managers and stakeholders also agreed that all forward thinking ideas needed to be reviewed and decided upon with appropriate speed and precision, which brought me a great sense of satisfaction and accomplishment. Although this situation did not directly affect the succession plan, it magnified the importance of having a management procedure in place to handle urgent and important issues that can impact a company's future bottom line.

But when a roadblock to succession planning seems insurmountable, I encourage all parties to recommit to the process. There are always answers to problems, but they just need to be discovered. Time, dedication, and the willingness to open ourselves to new ideas or compromise are embedded in the private business culture. Consequently, I find that when the things get tough, entrepreneurs by their very nature find a way out of the dilemma.

Another attribute found in entrepreneurship regularly embodies the culture of trial and error. Experiments to find better ways to do a task are continuous and result in keeping what works and discarding what doesn't. To be successful, you have to accept rejection. A mentor of mine put it this way: "You'll never get the sales order, unless you ask for it."

Ironically, I later became more persistent in my sales approach after a friend told me a story about my father. He said that my Dad would never take no for an answer unless he heard it three times from a prospect. That made a great deal of sense to me, and I reformulated my view of the subject. Ever since then, I think of sales this way: you just rephrase your offer the second time and then reposition your request the third time. If the answer is still no, the sales opportunity does not exist and you must move on. Those rules also apply to a succession plan.

Strategic planning objective in a small business environment can be traumatic so imagine for a moment that you have just been diagnosed with a serious illness. Then further imagine that it is your business has been diagnosed with a serious problem. As the entrepreneur, you probably would ask the following questions:

> How do I cash out now?

> What can I do to correct the problem?

> Who should I blame?

Optimism tells us to select the second option. Reality and prudence might lend us to select first, and weakness could direct us toward the third. We all know there is no perfect answer to this exercise. Each individual addresses a situation differently. Depending on one's viewpoint and personality traits, any of the three options could be correct. My point, as it relates to flexibility, is to be cognizant of the human condition.

Entrepreneurs have strong viewpoints, and at times will stick to their conviction beyond reason. That's what makes them so refreshingly unique and necessitates the use of a technique that I referred to as "tabling." When an adjustment needs to be made and the sure stubbornness of the parties becomes apparent, we must simply put the issue aside temporarily. I prefer to use tabling as a solution whereby the key issue is not lost in committee but rather given more time for consideration in what, hopefully, will be a non-emotional state.

This approach may seem counterproductive, but I have put the brakes on the decision-making process and found it to be very effective. I've put an issue aside during a meeting just briefly, only to bring it up again a few minutes later when people have had an opportunity to either think—or joke—about the issue. It's all about timing, yours and theirs, and this technique can be highly successful in diffusing emotional issues if used properly and sparingly.

Preparation is also vital to the succession process. While participating in a pension group known as the Retirement Administrators and Designers of America (RADA), I learned early in my career from a mentor named Carlton Cook of Birmingham, Alabama, to always prepare for any meeting. His particular technique was the use of a simple typed agenda in a clear outline format. He insisted on presenting the agenda to a prospect or client as the meeting began for three reasons:

> It focused Carlton's thoughts in preparation for the meeting.

> It helped him control the meeting and kept the emphasis on important issues.

> It demonstrated to the client that he was organized and knew the subject matter.

Likewise, business owners should be more organized and set better priorities in succession planning through the use of agendas. Even a handwritten one demonstrates organization and the fact that you've actually thought about a specific topic. The extra step of a typed agenda can add instant credibility. It also easily allows for "tabling" since all participants can clearly see that particular agenda item has been bypassed or eliminated.

Throughout the arch building process, G-1 and G-2 should be openly sharing new information and communicating expectations. Consequently, this dialogue and commitment to the process should lead to changing leadership roles that result in greater productivity, stability, and firmness during the assembly of the plan. There also will be a noticeable change in behavior if done properly. The participants will absorb new data and will react to the information with more sensitivity because they're no longer outsiders and are actively involved in a particular issue. To help parties come to consensus, I openly encourage them to develop their thoughts from three points of view:

> How will the issue impact you?

> How will it affect the other party?

> How will that change impact "us"?

The dynamics of interpersonal relationships are complicated and may need to be sorted out by trained professionals if issues are too turbulent and create too much anxiety for all parties, especially when there is a history of poor communication between parent and child that hinders succession planning and related exercises.

We sometimes find that to be the case when an obstacle such as knowing that as a child a successor had Attention Deficit Disorder (ADD) with a lack of concentration, short attention span, and impulsiveness. This creates extra stress for everyone because these developmental problems in children often carry over into the intergenerational discussion of adulthood. What complicates meaningful communication further is the fact that some disorders are inherited.

Dyslexia is a common learning disability. It interferes with learning sounds and reading despite average or above average intelligence, adequate motivation, educational opportunities, and normal eyesight and hearing. I found an unusually insightful quote on this subject from a column by James E. Barrett in the Spring 2002 issue of *Family Business*:

> "Those who suffer from Dyslexia and ADD often exhibit greater ability to think outside the box than their supposedly 'normal' colleagues. Einstein and Edison were dyslexic."

When working with unique entrepreneurial minds, we must allow for a balance between structure required in a business and the ability to be flexible in order to adapt to individual personalities and family dynamics. We must have a sturdy structure yet allow for modification. Think of a tall oak tree known for its slow growth and hard wood. The branches are flexible and bend with the wind, but if they are too stiff they will break.

Fortunately, G-1 and G-2 always agree they must be flexible in succession planning when it comes to the federal tax structure because it changes so frequently and makes wealth transfer a challenging task. Take, for instance, the estate and gift provisions in the Economic Growth and Tax Relief at Reconciliation Act of 2001. The applicable exclusion amount that is not subject to estate tax was $1.5 million per person in 2005 and $2 million per person in 2006-2008.

Then the amount changes to $3.5 million for 2009 until the estate tax is repealed for one year in 2010. Thereafter, the applicable exclusion amount is one million per person, and wealth in excess of the applicable exclusion is subject to a progressive estate tax. Without question, the only things constant in life are death and taxes, and private business owners must plan for both.

∞　∞　∞　∞

Two points I earlier made in Chapters Five and Six need to be reiterated at this juncture: by addressing issues that bring uncertainty in an orderly fashion and by creating contingency plans for crises, we have placed solid and stable blocks in your planning arch. Now, by being flexible, we have bought time to rearrange essential items in the arch and increased the likelihood of completing the arch and the succession plan. Two excellent examples:

A first-generation client approaching retirement had completed the first four steps of a succession plan and was content. He had also just funded a buy/sell agreement with his son and was comfortable with his successor's development. Then business boomed and new opportunities emerged that could take his revenues to a significantly higher level. With mutual agreement of his successor, the owner postponed the transfer and bought time to efficiently grow the business. He, however, continued to work on the orderly transfer of his responsibilities to the successor in preparation for the day that he would leave the business.

In another case, a founder did the opposite by deciding to quickly complete the plan because of the promises he made to his son and a key employee to relinquish ownership and operational authority.

CHAPTER EIGHT

REALITY CHECK

By now, the owner and successor have probably leaned on specially trained professionals and worked hard to solve individual issues for the good of the succession process. I've discovered that also means there's a good chance fatigue may have manifested itself among all parties.

The enormity of the succession process as well as the reality of what will follow really takes hold of G-1 and G-2, and it is at this point that succession planning generally succeeds or fails. As a model below indicates, the blocks of The McCabe Arch grow closer, and the momentum towards completion builds.

Reengagement Plan
- Will activities and hobbies really make the retirement fulfilling?
- Prepare to exit.

Shouldering the Weight
- Successor leadership responsibilities grow.
- Industry contacts develop.

Family, Management Consultants & Social Workers

Founder   Successor

Copyright ©2004 Harry M. McCabe
All rights reserved

But often the fear of the unknown becomes apparent in one or both generations. They are in uncharted territory and frequently hesitate to move forward because they simply have never been down this path before in their lives. It's human nature. If you don't know what your next step is, you are not likely to take it.

So the fifth phase of the 7 Steps to Succession℠ becomes an old-fashioned reality check of personal goals and aspirations for the owner and successor, and open communication becomes the most essential factor in the succession planning process.

I learned this lesson long ago from a colleague who told me that while counseling an executive approaching retirement he conducted joint meetings with the owner and his spouse. Each described their expectations during retirement. My colleague excitedly explained how the husband wanted to improve his golf game and dedicate significant time to the local church. This seemed quite reasonable.

However, his wife explained that she had been waiting twenty-five years for her husband to retire so he could finish the basement remodeling project, and the disconnect between husband and wife became apparent.

I find these disconnects occur when I challenge G-1 founders to stretch their thinking and state their real objectives. Actually, this exercise starts in the second step of my succession process in financial terms, and I build upon it during this phase with emotional issues. We must get them to give a clearer vision of the next phase of their life. It could be a new career, or it could be retirement. Activities stemming from their hobbies, involvement with a not-for-profit board of directors, or other leisure activities such as taking dream vacations are just a few of the many options that may consume more of their time. They must get excited about engaging in the next phase of life and prepare to let go of the business.

Once, a founder wrote in his "re-engagement" plan that he needed to make sure that the successor took more weight off him so that he could have the time and energy to accomplish more of his hobbies. The founder seemed weary. I suspected the business had become a burden, and he longed for retirement.

During this transition period, the founder may also feel less needed or less able to contribute to the success of the business. Or perhaps he feels that a world full of technology is moving too fast, and he cannot keep up. Maybe the *fun* of running a business has vanished because of the aging process. Without question, declining health contributes to the difficulties during this transition in late adulthood.

The vision that provided the drive and ambition during the owner's early and middle adulthood for the business might now be in better focus and not as glamorous as originally conceived. After a lifetime of planning and organizing, an owner may view the creation of a plan for the next phase of life as a mundane and downright boring task. The reasons for a lack of clarity at this stage are varied, depending on the personal commitment, success, and happiness experienced by the founder during the course of establishing and growing the company.

I was taught early in my career during a study group that if we were to implement any of the new ideas that we learned while attending the annual conference that **"you have to stop doing something *old* before you can start doing something *new*."** This is a profound statement, and I apply it when I coach entrepreneurs going through change at the end of their career.

Predictably, greater reflection and clearer direction often occurs when the founder begins to practice retirement activities. For three decades, I watched many of my most successful Chicago and Midwest clients avoid the cold and snow and take extended winter vacations in warmer climates. As a young pension consultant, I regularly saw the phenomenon. The cycle began when the first generation needs to get away from the business and take *any* sort of vacation. They could only afford to be away from the office for a short time since they did not have any competent successor or management team in place yet. Typically, they were young entrepreneurs with a growing firm.

Sometimes, they knew they had to take time off and would vacation at a ski resort in Michigan or northern Wisconsin. Other times, they attended an industry annual meeting and took a few extra days as a vacation. These events were usually held in a warmer location, but the time spent away from the office would still be limited to a week or ten days maximum.

As the business matured and the company infrastructure improved, the owners took longer trips, with the second-generation son or daughter left to run the business. This gave them a great sense of peace since they knew someone from the family was in charge during their absence. Eventually, the owners bought property at their winter destination, and the winter getaways became a permanent second home. Time spent away from the office increased as they got older, and the second-generation gained more responsibility for the company, including marketing, client relations, and vendor contacts.

As I discovered during telephone conversations with the senior generation at their winter homes about financial decisions relating to the year-end investments and contributions to their retirement plans, they had access to all relevant business information. They received financial statements, production information, and employee-related internal data. Additionally, they conducted personal meetings with key clients at their winter retreats and made major strategic decisions while on vacation while tactical decisions were left to their sons and daughters back home in Chicago.

By witnessing this cycle, I determined many critical business and family functions developed simultaneously, especially the concept of real versus perceived authority and overlapping family dynamics. Examples:

Frustration from the second-generation developed occasionally during these extended times of separation. A daughter, for instance, felt disconnected from her parents and unable to discuss an issue needing resolution and made what she considered the correct decision by firing an employee. A few months later, her father returned to the office and learned the effect the dismissal had on a particular client. He rehired the ex-employee without consulting with his daughter. The decision devastated her and impaired her ability to deal with delicate personnel issues.

The second example pertained to a vendor relationship. While his parents took their winter vacation, a son wanted to buy a new copy machine. The vendor refused and said, "Why don't we wait till your Dad gets back?" In the eyes of the vendor, true authority still rested in the founder.

These situations clearly demonstrate how difficult succession planning can be when the second-generation is overshadowed by the more dominant senior generation. If small decisions can't get made without clear lines of authority, imagine how frustrating the successor feels about trusting a parent to relinquish real control of the company.

The second-generation also is expected to carry the weight of the daily operations and keep cash flow moving positively when the first-generation is away on holiday. This escalates into a huge responsibility and becomes crucial as the succession plan is developed because G-2 must prove that the business can turn a profit under his/her supervision. Cash flow projections must be attainable and credible to both banker and the departing shareholder. The banker, especially, wants to make sure outstanding loans and additional funding for the sale of the company to the successor are secure.

The structure of an internal sale will be made up of numerous components. As indicated earlier, company real estate and office leases are the two most common. The first generation may keep land that the company owns and receive cash flow for retirement income in the form of lease payments. There may also be a "non-compete" clause included in the consulting agreement, and payments for this covenant may be expanded over a number of years. We often find the transfer of stock may include payment in the form of a loan with a long-term repayment schedule.

BOTTOM LINE: A BUSINESS MUST BE PROFITABLE TO MEET THESE OBLIGATIONS AND GENERATE THE APPROPRIATE CASH FLOW. THE SENIOR GENERATION RECOGNIZES THIS RISK AND WILL NOT LET GO UNTIL THESE FUTURE PAYMENTS ARE REASONABLY ASSURED. THIS, OF COURSE, MEANS THE SUCCEEDING GENERATION MUST DEMONSTRATE THE ABILITY TO LEAD THE COMPANY IN A PROFITABLE MANNER.

When we overlay the family dynamics such as a father/son, or mother/daughter relationship and the informal lines of communication, the situation gets even more complicated. The father may be the official boss in the company, occupy the corner office, and own the majority of voting stock. But when the father and mother try to influence all the activities of the next generation, the successor rightly perceives overwhelming pressure. I frequently come to the conclusion that the *real* challenge for the successor is to shoulder the *wait* for the day the owner relinquishes control of the company.

Growing up in the shadows of a strong personality can be very difficult for a successor. Just ask me. When I returned from the Army and went to work at Consolidated Pension Consultants after my father had passed away, I often heard the comment "the apple doesn't fall far from the tree." His business colleagues and clients, friends of the family, and others delivered this comment to me from different perspectives. I, however, always took it as a complement since I respected my Dad and felt that anyone who compared me favorably to him said a good thing. I was more or less a living memorial to him.

Throughout my working career, I also observed sons and daughters of business owners who had more difficulty with this comparison. I surmised that it was due to an ever-shifting, real-life daily challenge for young adults to fill their father's shoes and never quite got it right. To make matters worse, their parents continued to place higher and loftier goals on them and still continued to critique their actions. I had many conversations with successors about this phenomenon and responded this way:

It is true that the apple doesn't far fall from the tree. However, the young sapling needs sunshine to be able to grow strong and straight. If the preceding generation casts too large of a shadow, than the sapling will either perish or grow up crooked as he strives to find his own sunlight. Both generations need to be cognizant of this. I recommend that the senior generation pare back some of its branches, pruning some of its responsibility, and allowing enough sunlight to reach the offspring so he or she can grow properly. This trimming activity might need to be a large wedge carved from the branches of the tree, allowing both generations to stand tall side-by-side.

A knowledgeable owner recognizes the negative impact of impatience and delays in passing control of the company. By completing his "re-engagement" plan in a timely manner, G-1 vastly increases the chance that the company will be successfully transferred to a successor and that both owner and successor will be happily entrenched in their new roles.

But before the process is complete, the successor must also apply the adage of "you have stop doing something *old* before you can start doing something *new*." He must make the transition from follower to leader. I personally experienced implementing this advice from my senior RADA study group member Jack Scott of Columbus, Ohio.

Later, I learned firsthand what it really meant to lead my own company after I established Retirement Program Corporation. I was on my own and did not have the advice of either my Dad or Uncle George from across the hall. But I needed to develop my own contacts throughout the financial industry to find technical information and current, accurate knowledge about retirement plan administration. I also found management consulting resources to supplement my legal and tax advisors.

This challenge holds true for any potential G-2 owner. When he occupies the corner office, he should have a support group in place to give him advice and assistance for general business practices and emergencies. Ultimately, G-2 must assume the mantle of leadership and accept full responsibility for his decisions.

At the fifth phase in the succession process, the successor must demonstrate leadership and recognize the transitional needs of owner. Slowly but surely, the leadership role in the company will tip towards the second-generation. The balance is delicate. By shouldering the weight and lifting certain burdens from the founder during the fifth phase of 7 Steps to Succession[SM], the successor undergoes the ultimate reality check and will be in excellent position to complete the process.

CHAPTER NINE:

PUT IT IN WRITING

Documentation becomes extremely important as we reach the latter stages of the succession planning process, so it's time to move from notepaper and pencils with erasers to formal documents and pens!

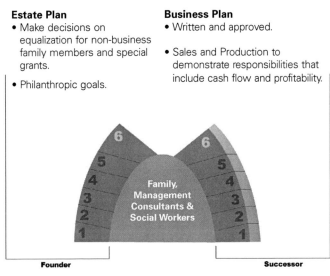

Estate Plan
• Make decisions on equalization for non-business family members and special grants.

• Philanthropic goals.

Business Plan
• Written and approved.

• Sales and Production to demonstrate responsibilities that include cash flow and profitability.

Family, Management Consultants & Social Workers

Founder

Successor

Copyright ©2004 Harry M. McCabe
All rights reserved

For the successor, this phase of the 7 Steps to Succession^{SM} process includes the use of the written business plan. Concurrently, the owner might revamp his estate planning documents. These activities formalize strategic planning components and leads directly to the final documentation needed for an eventual smooth transfer of the business. The succession planning process has reached a critical step. Without formal documentation, various interpretations and misunderstandings of the deal can—and probably will—create unnecessary errors and even hard feelings.

I find this aspect of succession planning fascinating because it intertwines complex strategies and products with the need to simplify and explain the issues clearly so both generations can understand the implications and then compare the results to their personal objectives. Both owner and successor must come to the table to openly share their written plans.

Equally important, special advisors continue their activities but from different perspectives. The attorney/client privilege is unique and, hopefully, lawyers will help rather than hinder the process. Succession planning components must now fit together, and the technical expertise of the advisors must strive for an inter-locking effort for the eventual achievement of the stated mission.

If the advisor is paid on a transaction basis, i.e. a commission is paid at the closing of a transaction, the advisor may provide the sustaining momentum to bring the strategy together and keep the process going until conclusion. To be sure, a properly trained life insurance agent can be a valuable member of the estate planning team. This is similar to how the business broker works when a sale is made to an outside third-party because a decision was made not to pass the company to an internal party. The broker receives the commission only when the sale is completed.

However, the cost associated with high hourly billing rates of advisors to the owner may cause him to pause and even postpone strategy development. At this stage of the game, it is important to assess and properly align the compensation of advisors to make sure the expense does not further delay or stop the succession planning process.

On the right side of the arch, the second-generation must complete a detailed business plan. It must be comprehensive and include reliable pro forma projections of cash flow for at least three-to-five years. Developing a business plan is critical for continued growth and success because it serves as a tool to help the successor collect and organize thoughts, gain feedback from the current owner, and guide future business decisions.

A new advisor might be brought in at this point to assist in the creation of a customized planning guide to meet the specific needs of G-2. Overall, I have found that multigenerational firms that have a business plan tend to have more revenue and profit growth than those businesses that do not have a plan.

The scope must include these major provisions:

> Purpose of plan;

> Personal goals of ownership;

> Business structure, Mission and Vision;

> Market opportunity and strategy;

> Optimal client;

> Services, products, and business model;

> Service model;

> Financial goals;

> Marketing and operations.

Then key internal employees and external providers/vendors should review the written business plan and provide feedback as necessary. This procedure usually builds trust and faith among all parties impacted by the eventual transaction. For example, I have witnessed a non-family executive in a family business critique the anointed successor's written plan. The review process presented him with a chance to preview the new authority's objectives, anticipate its implementation, and understand the management style. Consequently, he gained confidence in the new owner's leadership capability and expressed a willingness to accept some of the changes.

At this juncture, the successor's core values also need to be reaffirmed. His mission statement and vision of the business portrayed in the business plan allow all to draw conclusions about the future direction of leadership.

I've also observed and noted the response of other advisors after reading the details of the business plan. For instance, a banker will undoubtedly react when a line of credit for the business needs to be extended after transfer of ownership. This vital component of the financial strength in a continuing business enterprise cannot be overlooked when certain existing assets are pledged as collateral to secure the line of credit or other properties are mortgaged with long-term financing. The first-generation can't exit the business if his name is still on the note.

The implications are immediately recognized. The exact titling of assets must be clearly understood, which naturally triggers a review of the estate plan of the senior generation. G-1's estate plan should include, at the absolute minimum a Last Will and Testament as well as separate Power of Attorney documents for health and property.

During the review, we also draw upon information from second phase of the succession planning and update it if necessary. Perhaps members of G-2 have gotten married and grandchildren have joined the family as a new generation. On some of my planning assignments, I have found that a grandchild may have special needs, and the grandparents feel compelled to set aside assets for the support, training, and medical attention that the child will require.

Other times, the arrival of grandchildren presents an opportunity for G-1 to put aside extra funds specifically for the funding of their college education and includes restrictions on when and how the funds can be distributed. The focus of this planning should be to supplement the succession planning process and use various multigenerational wealth transfer techniques.

If warranted, revocable trusts for privacy and an Irrevocable Life Insurance Trust (ILIT), as required for ownership of a first and or second-to-die life insurance policy, will be adopted at this level of planning.

Other more sophisticated instruments include intentionally defective grantor trusts, family limited partnerships, and grantor retained annuity trusts. All advisors to the owner must coordinate their efforts to select the appropriate planning instruments. In the documentation process, we try to accomplish an orderly living consumption of wealth plan that provides adequate cash for current spending, tax payments, gifting, and contingencies as well as the eventual distribution of the wealth to future generations, special bequeaths, and payment of estate taxes.

The estate planning discussion and revisions to documents or creation of new entities must include both husband and wife. Similarly, the plan must be reviewed for alignment with the core values and beliefs of G-1 that were completed at the beginning of the 7 Steps to Succession[SM] process to ensure future planning implications will be congruent with current beliefs. This step solidifies past thinking and confirms that the revised plans fit well into The McCabe Arch and for G-1.

It is important to note that provisions for charitable interests can be detailed or revised at this point. Tax laws and regulations clearly encourage support for not-for-profit and charitable organizations, and the Internal Revenue Code gives generous deductions from the calculation of federal income taxes for contributions to qualifying recipients.

A Charitable Remainder Trust (CRT) may provide G-1 with an income stream from the sale of a highly appreciated business asset, could eliminate immediate capital gains tax, and may qualify as a charitable income tax deduction. Briefly, an attorney assists in establishing the CRT and transferring of the ownership of the highly appreciated asset to the CRT. G-1 also receives a charitable income tax deduction based on the calculated value of the remaining interest in the gift to the charity.

The trustee of the CRT then sells the highly appreciated asset, not incurring capital gains tax on the sale and reinvests the proceeds in income producing assets. Depending on how the income stream from the CRT is structured, G-1 could receive taxable income from the CRT for life, the combined joint life with spouse, or a specified term not to exceed twenty years. When the income stream terminates, the remaining assets in the CRT are distributed to a charity.

But the whole concept of charitable giving can be time-consuming and confusing. I vividly recall being in an advanced charitable planning presentation while attending an annual meeting of the Association for the Advancement of Life Underwriting (AALU). During a break, I stood in the hallway with a fresh cup of coffee discussing the CRT concept with other attendees. Then one of them nonchalantly said that these philanthropic ideas only work if clients like to give their money to charity.

The comments seemed somewhat unusual but basic. However, upon further reflection, I remembered real-life situations where my client definitely liked the tax impact and positive cash flow results, but frankly, had no charitable intentions in his core values. Unfortunately, we wasted a lot of time discussing this option and analyzing projections when the key element of giving assets to charity would never occur.

In another planning situation, I was involved with a family that had a long tradition of tithing. There truly existed a commitment. When it came time to gift a valuable parcel of land, the time and expense that went into making it happen was well worth it. We made sure that the proper valuation and gift tax calculations were done to protect against future scrutiny from the Internal Revenue Service.

Effective August 17, 2006, anyone 70½ and older can make an IRA rollover gift to a qualifying charity of up to $100,000. This direct rollover can be ideal for disposition of qualified assets that will not be needed to support the retiree's lifestyle. This technique can avoid the punitive tax imposed by a violation of Required Minimum Distribution rules. Further, the change helped to eliminate a concern for estate taxes since the donor was no longer entitled to the donated portion of the IRA.

Initially, these assets were troublesome from a planning perspective because they could not be typically gifted away and were still subject to income tax on withdrawal. But special care needs to be used with this provision. If it is not extended by further federal legislation, it will expire at the end of 2007.

A different technique, the Grantor Retained Annuity Trust, allows G-1 to retain an income stream from property transferred to a trust for a defined time period. It eventually excludes the property from the taxable estate. The beneficiaries of this irrevocable trust, however, can be family members.

Provisions for offspring and relatives not included in the business must be considered. "Estate equalization" between children with the proper alignment of beneficiary designations can easily be adapted with both basic and advanced planning techniques. The real question from an emotional and financial standpoint becomes, "Is equal fair?"

Given the ever-changing federal tax legislation as a result of the aforementioned Economic Growth and Tax Relief and Reconciliation Act (EGTRRA) of 2001, it is imperative to review the formulas embedded in estate planning documents. Many states have also uncoupled their inheritance tax formulas from the federal calculation due to the 2001 law, so special attention must be given to state tax implications.

We also must counsel the first-generation on the orderly consumption of various assets that they have accumulated. Often, the original perception of someone approaching retirement is to retain the principal and just live off the interest. I have found this wish unrealistic for many individuals. We must prepare for cash flow that might be generated from long-term leases of real estate, principal and interest payments on notes as a result of the sale of stock, and other employment related deferred income that might be due upon retirement.

Future cash flow and the suspected tax impact must be layered onto projections of personally held portfolios of stocks, bonds, and other marketable securities that will generate income and capital gains. Of course, IRAs and pensions must be taken into account as well as Social Security benefits.

It is my feeling that even more needs to be done. Active planning beyond provisions for death and orderly transfer of assets prior to death must include Social Security benefits as well as funding for long-term illness or disabling accidents. With annual nursing home costs in 2005 at $66,000 and projected at $200,000 in 2030, long-term care costs can be daunting.

Additionally, the cost of home care that provides assistance with bathing, dressing, meal preparation, transferring, and light housekeeping will continue to escalate for an aging population.

This ever-changing environment often frustrates the entrepreneur. The cost for professional advice coupled with the time needed to review and decide on alternatives drains financial and emotional resources, and the process becomes too confusing and overwhelming. Therefore, planning for the ultimate distribution of wealth and an estate is not a high enough priority, so planners and advisors resort to a few failsafe techniques.

One of the most common planning devices for a married couple allows for each individual to take advantage of their estate tax exclusion under federal law. To make this work, sufficient assets need to be exclusively titled to the party (either directly or through revocable trusts) and coordinated with other provisions of the Will or designation of beneficiary for trust property and life insurance policies.

∞ ∞ ∞ ∞

Another component is a Credit Shelter Trust (CST), also known as the bypass trust. At the death of a spouse, specific designated assets totaling $2,000,000 for 2007-2008 can be transferred to the trust without incurring estate tax. The balance of the estate assets, if transferred to the surviving spouse, is not subject to estate tax either, since transfers to the spouse qualify for the estate tax unlimited marital deduction.

This technique worked perfectly for my family. After my mother died in 1991, I personally experienced the trials and joys of wrapping up the affairs of a loved one. She appointed me to be the executor of her estate in her will. The effort was minimal as her personal holdings were in order, and Probate Court approved the distribution of her assets. My siblings all assisted with the division of her personal effects without any arguments and supported each other emotionally.

As noted in Chapter Six, part of my father's plan involved the use of a bypass trust. The residual value of the trust at Mom's death amounted to just over $400,000. This did not have to go through probate nor was it subject to estate tax, since Mom never had control over the trust. A local bank was trustee. After her demise, I suggested that the bank be removed as trustee to ease the administration and reduce the fees. I became the successor trustee, to prepare the final distributions. Under the trust terms, each of Dad's five children would receive one-fifth of the remaining value.

Shortly after mailing out the final checks, I received a telephone call from my youngest sibling, Mary Ann. My recollection of our phone conversation still brings tears to my eyes. Mary Ann explained that she didn't feel like she needed funds from Dad, in part, because she felt she had received more than her fair share of family wealth as a result of her inheritance from Mom in addition to Social Security benefits prior to her reaching a majority age.

She went on to explain that her older siblings, including me, could use the money for mortgage payments and other costs associated with raising young children. Finally, she became a bit panicky about squandering the funds.

Dad loved her, and my job was to convey this to her in a meaningful way. I explained that the check represents a gift to her from Dad. Although many years had past, he wanted her to have this money to use as she wanted.

∞ ∞ ∞ ∞

Yet another vehicle to provide liquidity entails the use of an Irrevocable Life Insurance Trust (ILIT). A life insurance policy with death proceeds free from income taxation and owned by an ILIT is not subject to estate taxes and provides a mechanism to create wealth in a tax efficient manner. Often, estate planning ends with the use of the ILIT and does not proceed into the wealth transfer of the family business, since the rationale of providing enough liquid assets upon the demise of the shareholder provides the solution.

An even more sophisticated estate planning technique is a Family Limited Partnership (FLP). Family members establish a FLP as a business entity and define the arrangement that can help facilitate the transfer of assets from one generation to the next. A FLP can accomplish two things: 1) transfer assets between generations without giving up total control until a desired point in time, and 2) freeze the value of the business or assets belonging to the FLP.

In most cases, the parents are the general partners and will transfer limited partnership interest to their children (or a child's trust). Because the net worth of the FLP interests, subject to the limitations on sales, are worth less than the underlying assets owned by the FLP, this transfer can result in a valuation discount of between 30 and 35%.

The FLP can be an effective way to transfer interests in a business from one generation to the next. If, for example, there is more than one business or the family owns several pieces of real estate, everyone will share equally in everything instead of choosing who gets what. The parents are able to transfer interests in the family limited partnership via gifts to children who often are in a lower income tax bracket. Current income generated by the business would then be taxed at the children's lower income tax bracket.

As you can see, numerous approaches can be implemented. Each owner's situation is different and dictates who should be brought into the planning process. Estate attorneys, tax accountants, or similar financial consultants must be committed to working as closely as possible with the client as well as other special advisors to ensure succession objectives are achieved.

A humorous anecdote best describes the need for cooperation. The owner of a construction company once attended a seminar that explained the use of a FLP. He then called his financial planner to see if this approach would fulfill his goals. In turn, the planner called the client's estate planning attorney, who suggested a complex FLP with numerous children's trusts as members.

Simultaneously, the client's CPA was asked to comment, and she introduced another financial advisor who simply said, "Put all of the assets in joint tenancy with the wife, and purchase a large multimillion dollar second-to-die life insurance policy in an ILIT."

The client moved immediately on this second plan design. By the time the first team of advisors made their detailed recommendations, the owner simply said, "I've completed all of my planning."

CHAPTER TEN:

CLOSE THE DEAL

We are perilously close to the top of The McCabe Arch and completion of the succession plan is within reach. However, just as the Biblical figure Moses could see the Promised Land but could not enter, I have witnessed owners and successors get this far and fail to complete the succession plan for deep-rooted emotional reasons.

Consequently, the support team may bear added weight and does most of the heavy lifting so G-1 and G-2 can concentrate on the impact of the final succession plan design. Often, the sense that the end is near brings unanticipated and unexplained anxiety to various parties.

Let Go
• Issues openly completed with final action.

Final Documentation
• Legal and operational authority transferred.

Legal Counsel
Trained Advisor

Founder

Successor

Copyright ©2004 Harry M. McCabe
All rights reserved

Problems most frequently surface just prior to the *signing party* when numerous legal documents are prepared, reviewed, revised, and eventually presented for signature. I've personally been involved in this process, and it is a daunting experience especially for those who have never bought or sold a business. I, like most prudent business owners, have been taught to understand the full meaning of every document before signing it. Unfortunately, few people are capable of understanding all the detail associated with a complicated transaction, and at some point they must trust their legal counsel to make sure everything meshes with their stated goals in transferring the business.

The documentation may include but is not be limited to a bill of sale, transfer of stock certificates, long-term leases, indemnity declarations, non-compete clauses, consulting arrangements, and other creative instruments needed to intertwine with existing estate plans. The process may be especially burdensome for the successor because he might not have been through previous business or estate planning whatsoever.

As a succession advisor, it is my duty to respect the personal concerns of the client and get the individual to a comfort level required to execute all documents necessary to help close the deal. This is no easy task. On occasion, I've had a client read one relatively harmless phrase out of the stack of documents and question the necessity of its inclusion. Then he flatly refused to continue with the signing party, got up from the table, and left the room.

I caught up with him at the elevator and asked for a private meeting to review his concern. Frankly, the client lost focus of the Big Picture. After an hour of emotional discussion, he returned to the signing party in a much more comfortable manner ready to execute the deal with all needed signatures. Finally, the tenseness evaporated, and father and son shook hands as businessmen and then embraced as loving family members.

In other circumstances, recognition of the financial impact of the transaction can slow down the closing process. Reviewing the figures a final time, a successor may question the underlying economics of the deal when it's time to sign the check, authorized the wire transfer, or sign a long-term note. With the proper presentation, explanation, and preparation of the deal's impact by a trusted advisor, the successor's last minute questions can be answered allowing the deal to close.

That's not to say that every deal will close on the designated day. I've witnessed or heard about many delays due to emotional issues that overlapped the business transaction.

While having lunch recently with a corporate lawyer friend of mine, he explained a situation involving a seventy-year-old client who had spent his life building a $50 million business and was ready to sell it outright to a third-party through an investment banker. After months of due diligence, counteroffers, and negotiations by a team of lawyers from both sides, the closing day finally arrived.

My friend explained that he was with his client in a separate room for final questions and document review. After a brief discussion, the man sat at a table in front of all the pages marked for his signatures. As he took the pen, his hand shook and he could not sign the paperwork. My friend, who had gotten to know the client quite well, kept his client in the private conference room and made sure he was physically okay. Then he sent word to the deal team in the larger conference room just down the hall there was a slight delay, the client just needed additional time.

A short time passed while my friend counseled his client, and they even went out for a short walk and cup of coffee. The attorney and client returned to the private room. Once again, the seventy-year-old owner picked up the pen. His hand visibly shook, and he could not control the pen. The man looked up at the attorney and said, "I just can't do it." My friend recalled that his client simply was not ready to let his life's work be taken from him. The deal never closed. A few years later, the owner died with the multimillion-dollar business still in his possession, triggering a significant federal estate tax bill for his heirs.

The issue of letting go is a complicated one. At times, the entrepreneurial spirit, with its imbedded need for control, poses a difficult obstacle to overcome. As my late father–in-law often said, "Growing old is not for sissies." However, if we have taken the proper steps and developed a reasonable reengagement plan, we greatly improve the chance of the founder moving out of the corner office and engaging in meaningful activities that will make up the next chapter of his life.

Many forward-looking entrepreneurs can make the transition even easier by understanding life cycles. Just as the business has a cycle, so do we as human beings. Today's older Americans are expected to live longer and really do not want to stop working completely.

One of my favorite authors, Ken Dychtwald, writes about a concept he calls *practice* retirement and refers to aging entrepreneurs as Cyclic Lifestyle Pioneers. Additional education, finding true joy in life, and setting new goals are part of the cyclical process. In a successful succession plan, we need to leverage these capabilities in a positive manner. For example, gracefully moving a chairman of the board to a different position in the organizational chart often can be done with the "emeritus" title.

But this kind of change can, at times, be a problem for the successor as well as the retiring founder. I've seen some creative use of dotted lines connected to the founder that attempts to represent informal authority. It may signify the continued mentoring of a key employee, or it may ease the transition from active senior management when the personality of the individual is deeply entwined in the culture of the business.

BOTTOM LINE: THE CHAIRMAN EMERITUS CAN STILL POINT TO HIS VALUE TO THE COMPANY IN A TANGIBLE WAY AND SEE HIS NAME STILL INCLUDED IN THE ORGANIZATIONAL CHART.

Although the term *re-engineering* is somewhat overused today, it certainly applies to G-1 as he lets go. He realizes that closing the deal is not the end and that there will be additional challenges in the days ahead. Many owners who let go are happy that the burden of a business has been lifted from their shoulders. They feel a great sense of relief and recognize they finally will have the necessary time to devote to new and exciting opportunities in the next phase of their life.

The transition doesn't happen unless G-1 and G-2 work together to close the deal. I often asked them to reflect back to the day when G-2 was first learning how to ride a two-wheel bicycle. The parent, G-1, ran alongside holding the back of the bicycle seat, and the child, G-2, knew that he wanted to have control of the bike. G-1 eventually let go and proudly observed that the training mission was accomplished. It just took the right balance and the right momentum for control to be passed from one generation to the other.

In succession planning, the process is reversed, and G-2 plays an important role in completing the final phase of The McCabe Arch. The successor needs to balance an aggressive tendency to take over that may appear to be an antagonistic push to the parent. Without doubt, the successor can taste the joy of freedom that comes with running, owning, and operating the business. He knows the deal will get done; he just wants to do it now. Therefore, he must supply force to keep the momentum going.

Getting the support of other family members to achieve his goal may be difficult, especially if other G-2 siblings feel the successor is getting too good of a deal. They may feel closed out of an opportunity and suffer from neglect. This friction must be overcome with open communications about the owner's estate and gift plan. Family dynamics are critically important, and timely input from the founder's spouse may help grease the machinery needed to resolve emotional and financial issues.

At the closing, I believe that the owner and successor should both have slight feeling that they gave away too much in the transaction. There should be an uneasy, subliminal sense that the other side won. If one side walked away with too much, the exchange would be lopsided. This mutual pressure supports a good deal and supports the placement of the keystone.

Planning Process Completed

The Key issues get resolved by agreement from both sides.
Support system can be removed to form the free-standing arch.

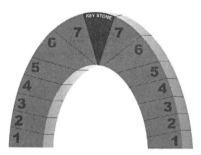

Copyright ©2004 Harry M. McCabe
All rights reserved

The founder and successor together firmly place the keystone in the center of the arch.

The arch is now finished and self-supporting, symbolizing the completion of the planning process. The custom-designed succession plan works specifically for the participating business and family.

For the founder, the completed arch may represent the door to retirement or the gateway to the next chapter of life. He experiences transition by passing under the arch opening and should be filled with hope and aspirations for future endeavors as well as a sense of peace and satisfaction for a job well done in leading the business for so many years.

For the successor, the completed arch symbolizes a front door to the business. He owns the company and possesses the keys to its future success. He must lead and grow the company.

The succession plan is complete, and the weight of The McCabe Arch is now balanced. The owner and successor contributed to the process, and all blocks of the arch are permanently in place to form an enduring testimonial.

But entrepreneurship is not for the feint of heart. Opening the business on the second of January every year tests the mettle of every business owner to accept the challenge of entrepreneurship. The jubilation of the prior year's success is history, the celebration short-lived.

He must do it all over again.

EPILOGUE

It only takes one generation to move a family business from a basement office to the Executive Directory of a skyscraper on LaSalle Street in Chicago. Just ask my Uncle George about the McCabe Family.

One day George, then thirty-three and a second-year agent working for Franklin Life Insurance, found himself on the corner of Monroe and LaSalle Streets in the Loop on a hot and humid summer day. He was between appointments with no place to go since he did not have an office. So he walked into the Harris Bank Building to find a public restroom to wash his hands and cool down. He found the air-conditioning a welcome relief. In the basement of the bank, he noticed the marble flooring, pleasant surroundings, and a reception desk for the bank's lockbox department.

Mr. O'Neil greeted George politely and asked if there was something he could do for him. George engaged him in a causal conversation and determined that there were fourteen private rooms where a customer of the bank could take a lockbox and privately review its contents. Mr. O'Neil explained that the cost was twenty-three dollars per year. So George rented a lockbox. A few days later, George returned downtown and brought along a few supplies in his briefcase.

Once again, Mr. O'Neil greeted George as he approached and assisted with obtaining the lockbox and escorting him to one of the private rooms. George put his insurance rate book and a few applications into the lockbox. George had also discovered a pay phone at the end of the hallway, where he could deposit a nickel and make outbound calls to various prospects and clients to confirm appointments.

This arrangement worked nicely for George because he could find a place to go between appointments, do paperwork, and even read the newspaper. Mr. O'Neil noticed the frequency of George's visits, and one day asked why he visited the lockbox so often. So George explained to Mr. O'Neil that, in effect, he used the lockbox private rooms as his office. Mr. O'Neil smiled and said "Son, with that kind of thinking, someday you're gonna' make a million dollars."

George became quite comfortable with his new office arrangement and even printed business cards with the following: "George C. McCabe, Insurance Broker, Harris Bank Building, Chicago." He continued to be respectfully received by Mr. O'Neil. At one point, though, a client asked why George didn't have a telephone number on his business card. George responded, "I'll call you before you ever have to call me!"

Later, a close friend wanted to see the lockbox operation. When George and Jack descended the stairs to the basement level and approached the reception area, Mr. O'Neil waived his hands and said, "Mr. McCabe, it's okay for you to use the private rooms, but you can't bring any clients into your office!"

Eventually, George gave up his downtown office when he was promoted at Franklin Life Insurance Co. Then he joined my father as they began Consolidated Pension Consultants Inc. and established an office on South Kedzie Avenue in Chicago.

Many years later, I took a sales position with an established insurance agency in downtown Chicago and explained that I needed my name listed on the building's Executive Directory. The firm, located at 135 S. LaSalle Street, agreed, and a few months later my name was placed in the directory. Then I invited Uncle George to visit me at the office, and we reminisced about his office next door in the basement of the Harris Bank Building.

The McCabe Family rose from the basement to the lobby directory in one generation as this 2003 photo illustrates.

George and Harry identified their Keystone, along with other members of the McCabe Family, and continue to celebrate the successful plan result.

∞ ∞ ∞ ∞

I love entrepreneurship and believe the tradition of free enterprise must be preserved. It is my hope that I have communicated the successes, challenges, and failures related to the transfer of a private business in an informative manner and that the techniques described in the 7 Steps to Succession℠ process help entrepreneurs pass a business on to their children.

The McCabe Arch is a tool to help simplify the complexities surrounding the American business owner, and it offers practical solutions for planning the orderly consumption and distribution of financial and emotional wealth.

I strongly urge any successful entrepreneur to complete the first four steps of the succession process. Creating a solid base with trusted advisors to address management issues, especially in crisis situations, generates real business value.

If the company is a start-up, the owner should have an eye toward his eventual exit from the business. On the other hand, a highly successful business owner, perhaps with multiple profitable enterprises, may repeat steps six and seven of my succession process if there are numerous family members, key employees, or outside buyers with different aspirations.

But the key to success in succession planning really occurs when an owner passes the spirit of entrepreneurship to all interested successors. With proper planning, the capitalist can pursue the God-given freedom to create a business and grow it, and then *Pass It On* to a worthy successor.

BIBLIOGRAPHY

Astrachan, Joseph H., Ph.D. *Family Business Review*. Boston, March 2003.

Bacharach, Bill. *Values-Based Selling*. The Art of Building High-Trust Client Relationships for Financial Advisors, Insurance Agents and Investment Reps. San Diego, 1996.

Barrett, James. *Family Business* magazine. Philadelphia, Spring 2002.

Brown, John H. *How To Run Your Business so You Can Leave It In Style*. Denver, 1997.

Copeland, Julie. *Family Business Magazine E-Newsletter*. November, 2006.

Dychtwald, Ken. PhD. *Age Wave*. The challenges and opportunities of an aging America. New York, 1989.

Frankenberg, Ellen PhD. *Your Family Inc*. Practical tips for building a healthy family business. Binghamton, New York, 1999.

Larson, Eric. *The Devil in White City*. New York, 2003

Leach, Peter. *Thisismoney.co.uk* Running a family business. March 2007.

Provident Life & Accident Insurance Company 1980 Annual Report. Chattanooga, Tennessee, 1981.

Shanker, M. C, & Astrachan, J. H. *Family Business Review*. Myths and realities: Family businesses contribution to U.S. economy. A framework for assessing family business statistics. Summer 1996.

The Bible–Deuteronomy 34:4.

www.2164.net. Andrea and Charles Bronfman Philanthropies